Piano

Owner's Manual and Buyer's Guide

Accordion

George Bachich

Copyright © 2012

George Bachich

All rights reserved

Published by Accordion Revival

P.O. Box 3238

Napa, CA USA

www.accordionrevival.com

ISBN: 978-0-9857045-0-6

The Piano Accordion Owner's Manual and Buyer's Guide *is dedicated to the new generation of accordion players now heralding a modern accordion revival. May you find as much fascination and derive as much pleasure as we have from this fabulous instrument.*

FOREWORD

An autopsy implies an intimate investigation; it literally means "to see for oneself." While it is a term often used to discover the reason and possible cause(s) of a person's death, this closely followed procedure when applied to an accordion, may, in fact, revive it so its bellows can breathe again. The miracle of that revival is why this book was written by my good friend and fellow accordionist George Bachich.

The unplayable and barely playable accordions are a pitiful sight, but George is the kind of person who is compelled to rescue, restore, and revive them to their former state of glory. With that goal in mind, and knowing he could not possibly revive them all by himself, his obsessive hobby became a calling to raise awareness and create a better informed public. His passionate (perhaps even evangelical) zeal, dedication, and fastidious attention to the smallest details have resulted in an accessible manual that anyone can use before buying an accordion.

There are hundreds, if not thousands, of accordions advertised for sale at accordion club meetings, on eBay auctions or Craigslist, and in some music stores where neglected, dusty, and homeless accordions await adoption. A glut of pre-owned accordions has always been displayed at the annual Cotati Accordion Festival, now in its 22nd year. Wading through this sea of old instruments in search of something useful can seem a bit daunting. Knowing how to evaluate a used accordion may save the buyer from the heartache of purchasing something unsuitable. This manual will prepare anyone, from novice to pro, with criteria for evaluating suitability in size, weight, quality, and overall health of any accordion.

In 2006 when I first met the author at the Accordion Club of the Redwoods (ACR), he was freely providing those services. Before, during, and after club meetings, he was performing minor miracles on the proliferating number of aging, and often ailing, accordions. Many had simply been abandoned on the shelf, others ignored and stored in their boxes, some were invaded by the usual organisms resulting from mildew, and almost all were viewed as 'not worth saving.' But some just needed a 'tune-up' so that a player could get more quality mileage. He educated owners about up-keep, offering suggestions and advice.

Soon after we met, the author and I worked together while I was Editor of the ACR newsletter. His stories and articles allowed even the non-musician to enjoy learning more about the beauty and mechanical parts of an accordion. George's exciting autopsies under the grille included more than just physical aspects. His thorough 'hands-on' understanding about reeds, switches, tone chambers, tuning, bellows, buttons, and keyboards, coupled with his knowledge gained from his first-hand interviews and visitations to Italian accordion factories in Castelfidardo, provided precious insights.

He helped others to recognize potential issues and problems, and he shared his expertise on how to evaluate and determine an accordion's true (and fair market) value.

It was becoming more apparent that accordion players, parents, teachers, and students, as well as potential accordion owners would greatly benefit by learning more about the criteria for buying, selling, and caring for the instrument. A new, improved accordion owner's operating manual was desperately needed.

Not since 1956 when O. Pagani & Bro., Inc. published an accordion repair manual (currently out of print) has there been a manual with the breadth, depth, and over-all knowledge on repair techniques, procedures, mechanisms, and servicing. Even if you own an accordion that needs no repairs, this *Piano Accordion Owner's Manual and Buyer's Guide* provides an exploration of various fascinating topics as well. You will come away from it fully appreciating and treasuring the accordion you own. Its well placed color photographs and diagrams prove the old adage that a picture is worth a thousand words by clearly illuminating and reinforcing the points made in the text.

I trust that this remarkable contribution to the history, maintenance, and continued successful revival of the accordion will provide many answers to the problems, questions, and issues that accordionists, teachers, students, and parents will encounter in their quest to find the accordion that is exactly right for them.

Sheri Mignano Crawford, Accordionist and Author
Petaluma, CA

CONTENTS

The accordion is a fabulous instrument, more versatile and capable than any other. Accordions can effectively accompany and complement practically any other combination of instruments, and are also one of the best solo instruments, easily serving as a one man band. Virtuoso accordionists thrill us with the power and beauty of the music they make with accordions.

However, accordions are not just for virtuosos, they are everyman's instrument. Accordions are easy enough to manage that anyone can learn to play simple, satisfying, beautiful music in their own home, even if they never intend to perform on stage. Accordions are alive; they breathe, they vibrate warmly on your chest, they are responsive to, and participate in generating mood and excitement, as they put forth full and magnificent chords, tones, melodies, all in a haunting timbre that draws us eagerly into the music.

All this makes it hard for me to accept how such a fine instrument could have suffered such an ignominious decline in popularity over the last half of the twentieth century. For cultural reasons, and through no fault of its own, the accordion fell from being a universally accepted multicultural icon to being an embarrassment, and the butt of snide and condescending jokes. Neglected in basements and garages for decades, the millions of accordions produced and sold in the United States between 1935 and 1970 slowly deteriorated, and many died.

But it's time now to bring those old accordions out and revive them. In just about every musical genre, creative artists are rediscovering that the accordion has a proper and meaningful role to play. Accordions appear on stage with the big stars, as well as in music videos and in TV commercials. Accordions are cool again. It's okay to have one now, and to admit that you play. Long dormant accordions are being brought back to life by long dormant accordion players bent on reclaiming the music they gave up decades ago. Life-long piano players are discovering the benefits of the accordion's versatility and portability, and are adding accordions to their stable of instruments. Younger generations, unaware of and unaffected by the oh, so yesterday notion that accordions might somehow be uncool, are embracing accordions as they deserve to be embraced.

As this modern accordion revival unfolds, the old instruments are being called back into service. They are coming out of the closet and finding their rightful places in living rooms, parks, restaurants, clubs, and even on stage.

This new interest in accordions creates a need for a book like this. Where else can people turn to find the information they need in order to participate in this revival? The only other books on this topic, as far as I have been able to discover, are either sadly outdated, maddeningly incomplete, or very poorly translated into

English. There are smatterings of useful information scattered around the internet, but there is currently no single source of up to date and readable information covering everything you need to know about owning and buying piano accordions. It is this gap that I have tried to fill.

I started repairing accordions about ten years ago, just as a hobby and as a way to keep my own accordions working properly. I was hesitant at first. Although mechanically inclined and normally accustomed to taking just about anything apart and figuring out how to fix it, I did not want to risk damaging such a delicate instrument. When my 50 year old accordion first came out of the closet and needed a little reviving, I took it to Smythe Accordions in Oakland, California for advice. Kimric Smythe very generously and graciously took me into his shop and allowed me to watch while he repaired it. He carefully explained everything he did as he worked, and showed me exactly how it was done, and suggested that I acquire a junk accordion to practice on before working on anything valuable.

I took his advice. I bought a hopeless piece of junk, ordered some supplies from Kimric, and went to work. Along the way I read everything I could find written about accordion repair, and talked to everyone I could find that had any experience repairing them. I found that very little had been written, and there weren't many people repairing them, but I picked up little bits of information here and there, and put everything I learned into practice on that old junker. Naturally, I learned the most by making mistakes and correcting them. When I had pretty much exhausted the possibilities on that accordion (it truly was not worth fixing), I bought a batch of 16 old accordions from a retiring dealer in Ohio and had them delivered to California.

As I began repairing them, I longed for some really expert advice on how to work more efficiently, exactly what tools and materials to use, and on where to find all the necessary parts and supplies, so I arranged a trip to Castelfidardo, Italy. I spent a full week visiting accordion factories, reed makers, bellows makers, keyboard makers, reed valve makers, and general parts suppliers. I was very well received everywhere. They ushered me around to all the work stations, allowed me to watch every stage of accordion manufacture, and graciously answered all my questions.

I could not have been happier. I returned home from the trip confident and invigorated, and began to spend even more time on accordion repair.

As word got out that I was repairing accordions, people in the local area began to bring their accordions to me for repair. I fixed anything they brought me, and never charged anyone. It was my hobby, I was still learning, and above all, I wanted to help them get their accordions back into action. But eventually, it got to be too much. There was obviously a lot of demand for accordion repair, especially free accordion repair, and I only had so much time, so I began to charge. Word continued to spread and people began to come from farther away. I took on more interesting repair jobs, tuning projects, and some complete rebuilds, and I got pretty good at it.

I began to sell some of the old accordions I had fixed up, and in that process discovered that my real goal is to help people find the accordion that is right for them, regardless of whether they buy it from me or from someone else.

People began to ask me for advice on what kind of accordion they should buy. They asked me to perform pre-purchase inspections of accordions they were considering, and appraisals on accordions they wanted to sell. A few began suggesting that I write a book to share with everyone what I had been sharing with them.

At last year's Cotati Accordion Festival (Cotatifest.com) the Golden State Accordion Club displayed a partially disassembled junk accordion, labeling it "Accordion Autopsy". I spent several hours standing over that accordion corpse answering questions and explaining to anyone interested just how it works, what often goes wrong, and what they should watch out for when buying an accordion. I enjoyed that so much that I offered to do it again this year, and I resolved to write this book for those whose interest may be stimulated by the accordion autopsy, and for everyone who owns or is considering owning an accordion. I hope you enjoy reading it.

George Bachich, May 2012

ACKNOWLEDGEMENTS

Writing this *Piano Accordion Owner's Manual and Buyer's Guide* has been fun, but I would probably never have made the commitment to do it if not for accordionist Pamela Tom, who saved all the explanatory emails I sent her in answer to her many accordion questions, and who urged me to include them in a book about accordions.

The final inspiration to write was provided by Carole Enneking and the Golden State Accordion Club by setting up the Accordion Autopsy, which made me realize how much I enjoy explaining accordions to anyone who will listen.

Sue Chan, Pamela Tom, Sue Hirigoyen, Jack Behseresht, and Sheri Mignano Crawford helped point me in the right direction by reviewing an early draft and telling me where it needed help.

Sheri led the way by forming Zighi Baci Publishing to self-publish her own books on *ballo liscio* and French *bal musette* music, which every accordion lover should have, and it was Sheri who urged me on whenever I had doubts about finishing.

My thanks go to all of them, to all the people who asked the questions that made me dig deeper to find the correct answers, and especially to Linda, my loving life partner of 40-odd years, for so graciously accommodating my accordion obsession.

George Bachich

INTRODUCTION

Accordions are all pretty much the same in terms of basic structure and operation. Any assortment of metal reeds tuned to the individual notes of the scale, an array of valves to direct air flow to individual reeds, a keyboard or two connected to linkages that open those valves, and a manual air pump to drive the reeds, all assembled into a compact unit you can hold in your hands or strap onto your chest, is probably an accordion.

However, accordions can vary greatly in the details. There are bi-sonic diatonic button accordions, monosonic chromatic button accordions, Russian bayans, concertinas, bandoneons, and piano accordions. Only the last category is treated here.

Even among piano accordions there is great variety, including many outlier designs and innovations that never caught on, and are therefore not the subject of this book. Such anomalies as the uniform keyboard, curved keyboard, angled keyboard, accordions playing in fifths rather than octaves, bass accordions (having only very low notes on the right side and no buttons at all on the left) may be great conversation pieces and museum exhibits, but they see little actual use in the real world, are not likely to be what you own or buy, and are therefore not what I want to explain.

I want to explain common piano accordions in a way that is easy for anyone to understand. I'm not writing about electronic accordions, midi accordions, reedless accordions or synthesizers. If those are your interest, this may not be the guide for you. But if you are interested in acoustic piano accordions, then you have my full attention. In the following pages I want to personally guide you through the available options and the factors to be considered when evaluating these options. When we finish, I want you understand how piano accordions work, how they differ from one another, and how to decide which one is right for you.

1.

Recognizing a Bargain

If you find a used accordion available for $300, is that a bargain? After all, new accordions cost several thousand dollars, so $300 for a used one sounds like a bargain, doesn't it?

As you might expect, it is probably not a bargain, but it all depends on the quality and condition of the instrument, how much you like it, and how much more work and money you are willing to put into it. This guide will help you evaluate used accordions and help prevent you from inadvertently paying more than you need to pay.

There are lots of accordions to choose from. Although there are probably only a few hundred thousand accordion players in the U.S., there are almost certainly several million accordions. Most accordion players own several, some own dozens, and even many non-players own one or two. That's because in the 1940's and 1950's, accordions were very popular, accordion schools were everywhere, and millions of American children learned to play.

In their heyday, accordions were produced and sold by the hundreds of thousands each year to meet this demand. The little town of Castelfidardo, Italy, had around 200 accordion factories in the 1950's and 60's, at their peak exporting around 200,000 accordions per year to the U.S. In addition, accordions were imported from Stradella, Italy, as well as from Germany, and there were many accordion factories in the U.S., as well. At the peak, about 250,000 accordions were sold in the U.S. in a single year. The vast majority of those accordions were student models, not of the highest quality, but surprisingly good for what they cost. Many of these are still around, most having been stored in closets, basements and garages, unused and slowly deteriorating for decades. When you see a used accordion for sale in a second hand shop, antique store, or on eBay, it is probably one of these.

The average accordion is about 60 years old, has not been played for decades, and has been stored in less than ideal conditions. Accordions are delicate complex instruments comprised of thousands of parts made from a variety of materials. Some of these materials are fairly durable, including aluminum, steel, wood, and plastic, but some are less durable, including cardboard, woven fabric, glue, varnish, felt, leather, and beeswax.

Time, disuse, cold, heat, moisture, and moths are the mortal enemies of accordions, causing wood to warp, cardboard bellows to mold, leather reed valves to curl, steel reeds to rust, aluminum parts to corrode, felt valve cushions to deteriorate, and glue, varnish, and wax to harden and crack. Depending on the extent of the damage, such an accordion may not even be salvageable, let alone a bargain. At the very least, it is likely to need several hundred or possibly even several thousand dollars in repairs.

So is $300 a bargain price for such an instrument? That obviously depends in part on what it will cost to put it in good condition. It also depends on what it will be worth *to you* once you have it in good condition, which is what I call *potential value*. This guide will help you evaluate the potential value of any accordion, as well as the likely cost to put it in good condition.

People have paid $300 or even a lot more for an accordion, only to find out later that the cost to repair it will exceed its potential value. Although uninformed buyers might pay several hundred dollars for an accordion like that, an informed buyer would assign it an "as-is" value of zero. We all want to be informed buyers, and this guide is intended to help make you one. To a knowledgeable buyer, *many used accordions are not bargains at any price*, and you will be better off if you learn to recognize and avoid those accordions.

Naturally, there are exceptions, and you are hoping to find them, or you wouldn't be reading this guide. I have found some, and if you are cautious, persistent, and well informed, you can find them, too. Once you understand how to compare one accordion to another, and how to anticipate what repairs they will need, you will be able to recognize the exceptions.

One of those exceptions was an accordion I rebuilt for a customer. He had paid around $200 for a great looking little accordion built in San Francisco in 1927. After inspecting it, I informed him that it was totally worn out, but that I could put it in top working condition if he wanted to put another $1800 into it. I told him the only problem was that when I finish, he will have spent $2,000 on an accordion that he might be able to sell for only $1,000.

Spending twice as much as you might expect to recoup in a sale may look like a bad deal, but I was not surprised when he said go ahead. Like me, he has an appreciation for non-monetary value, as well as resale value.

There is not really an established market for antique accordions, but to him the sentimental/historical value of this little accordion from 1927 eclipsed the dollar amount he might hope to get in a sale. It had real character, and would be a keeper, not for sale in any case, so the market value didn't matter much. The value in this kind of instrument lies in the pleasures of having it and showing it and playing it, not in the money you might get from selling it. Its potential value to him exceeded the cost of repair, so he paid me to rebuild it.

I underestimated the amount of time it would take me. I should have quoted much more than $1800 for that rebuild, so he got a good deal. However, I benefitted also, because rebuilding his accordion inspired me to look for a similar one for myself. I know from experience what a big job it is, but I want one anyway, so I bought one, and am in the process of rebuilding it. I will have a huge investment of time in it, with no hope of ever getting paid for all of it, but I don't care, because it's not for sale. My Piatanesi 1933 World's Fair Model is definitely a keeper.

Piatanesi 1933 World's Fair Model.

If you like funky old things and get a kick out of having something really old that works like new, this might be the kind of exception you are looking for. However, there are several other kinds of exceptions, some of which are less costly.

One of those other exceptions came to me in a bundle of 16

accordions I bought sight unseen from a retiring dealer for $100 each. They all needed work, and I bought them specifically to fix them up and sell them. As you would expect, some of them were pretty ratty, and will probably never be worth repairing. Some were so bad that I now use them for parts to repair others. A few I fixed up for sale, a couple I gave away, and one turned out to be an exceptional accordion, worth more to me than the amount I paid for the whole shipment.

It was unplayable when I got it. Someone had spilled a caustic solution on the bellows, which destroyed the leather seals in the corners of the bellows folds, so the bellows would not hold air.

However, the rest of the accordion appeared to be in excellent condition, so when I was visiting accordion factories and accordion component manufacturers in Castelfidardo, Italy, I ordered a new bellows custom made for it. When the bellows finally arrived, I installed it, and for the first time, heard the sweet sound of this instrument.

It sounded just right to me; wet, but not too wet (see chapter 5 for an explanation of "wet"); clear, but not too brassy. The bassoon reeds had a more resonant and mellow sound than any of my other accordions, and the reed response was better than most (although not as good as on a new Beltuna I played at the factory in Castelfidardo – more on that later).

At just 20 pounds, it was light and manageable. The 17 3/4 inch keyboard seemed to fit my hand perfectly. The bellows was deeper than on most ladies' size accordions (see Chapter 9), providing significantly more air.

The downside was that the keyboard action was too deep and the stiffest I have ever encountered, so I had to adjust all the key springs for a lighter feel and level the treble keyboard for shallower action. Another shortcoming was that the bottom connection for the shoulder straps was on the back of the accordion, up a few inches from the bottom, causing the shoulder straps to pinch into my armpits, so I moved the bracket.

After I fixed those problems, I found myself playing that accordion more and more. It soon became, and still remains my favorite accordion. The total cost was far in excess of the nominal $100 purchase price, but to me it is the best bargain I have ever found. My Lo Duca Soloist Console is definitely a keeper, not for sale at any price.

Lo Duca Soloist Console

I'm not suggesting that you run out and buy a Lo Duca. I have looked at several others of the same model, hoping to duplicate my favorite, but none of them has turned out to be quite as nice, proving that mine really is an exception, even among Lo Ducas. My point is that you, too, might stumble unexpectedly upon an exceptional accordion of any brand, and this guide is dedicated to helping you recognize it.

Another kind of exception came a few years ago at the Cotati Accordion Festival in California. One of the used accordion dealers there was packing up his unsold accordions at the end of the festival for the long drive home. I noticed a Giulietti Super in his inventory, but did not want to pay his asking price.

The Super was the top of the line Giulietti professional model, with double tone chamber (see chapter 6), handmade reeds (see chapters 11 and 25), and that fabulous deep sounding Giulietti bass. This one needed to have a few leathers replaced (see Chapter 16), but otherwise appeared to be in good condition. I already had a Giulietti Classic 127, which was the next model down, and wanted to upgrade, so I made him an eleventh hour offer of half what he was asking, thinking he might rather let it go for very little rather than haul it all the way back to Canada.

He explained that it was on consignment, and that to avoid hauling it back home, and to do his customer a favor, he would sell it to me for just what his customer had set as his minimum net price, with no dealer markup.

This was a few hundred dollars more than I had offered, but still a great bargain, considering the quality and reputation of the instrument, so I agreed. I think this was an exceptional deal because I have recently seen Giulietti Supers advertised for two or three times what I paid. Even though I originally considered the Super a keeper, if I can get that kind of money for it, I might sell it.

These exceptions to the rule are what we are all looking for, and I hope describing them helps you understand what I mean when I say that the definition of a bargain depends not just on initial price compared to potential market value, but also on what it will be worth *to you* once you put it in good condition. If an accordion has special appeal to you, it may be a bargain even if its total cost exceeds what other people might be willing to pay for it. This guide is designed to help you understand all the relevant features of accordions so you can decide which attributes you might find especially appealing.

I want to make it clear that I'm not copping out here. I will get around to estimating actual market value a bit farther on. But the important point for now is that the essence of any bargain is a price lower than value, and value can include nonmonetary factors. I'm telling these stories about exceptions I have found to help illustrate some of the factors you might want to consider when shopping for an accordion. This guide will explore all these factors, including the monetary factors, in much more detail in subsequent chapters.

The main two points to keep in mind are 1) All old accordions need repairs, so total cost always equals purchase price plus repair cost, and 2) As a buyer, you should address two questions: What will be its total cost, and what will it be worth to you once it is repaired?

The difference between these two numbers is the value to you of the accordion as is. If an instrument does not have special appeal to you, then you should stick to its "as-is" market value, which is the difference between what someone else would pay for it in good condition and the cost of putting it in good condition. Under this definition, the as-is market value of many used accordions is less than zero. It will often cost more to repair them than they could be sold for in good condition.

Of course, you can always go out and buy a new accordion. When I was in Castelfidardo visiting accordion factories I was completely blown away by the stunningly good reed response of the Beltuna Leader V Gold, Beltuna's top of the line acoustic LMMMH accordion, with tone chamber and handmade reeds by Artigiana Voce, one of Castelfidardo's larger reed manufacturers (see Chapters 4 and 5 for an explanation of LMMMH, see Chapter 6 for tone chambers, and see Chapters 11 and 25 for handmade reeds). I could play a four note chord with barely perceptible bellows motion. The reeds were so meticulously and perfectly voiced that the bassoon reeds began to sound at the same instant as the clarinet reeds, even under the lightest of bellows pressure (see Chapter 4 for an explanation of bassoon and clarinet reeds, and Chapter 11 for "voiced" and "voicing"). I was so pleased by this accordion that I would have bought it if the factory discount price had not been so high, the Euro equivalent of $10,000.00. That's a lot of money for an acoustic accordion.

I have to admit that I almost bought it anyway, but managed to restrain myself because, like you, I'm always hoping I can get what I want, or at least something very close, for a lot less money by shopping in the used accordion market.

So far, I haven't found it, but I think I may be getting close. I recently bought another Lo Duca Soloist Console on eBay, hoping to cheaply duplicate my favorite accordion. Unfortunately, on this latest one the reed response and sound quality are not as good as on my favorite (this is also true of several other Lo Duca Soloist Consoles that I have recently tested).

So I'm upgrading it. I bought a full set of handmade reeds from Binci in Castelfidardo for $1300, which I am installing in this latest Lo Duca. By the time I re-valve the treble and bass sides, refurbish the treble keyboard and bass machine linkages, and install a new bellows, I will have about $2,000 cash and another $3,000 worth of labor invested in it. In return for that investment I'm hoping to have the rough equivalent of a new Beltuna, at least in terms of the features I liked most about it. Was my $300 purchase price a bargain? I'm optimistic about that, but I won't know until I have it finished.

Of course, you have other options, as well. You can buy a reconditioned accordion from a reputable dealer. Naturally, you will pay a lot more than $300, but you won't have to make any costly repairs right away if the dealer has already made them. This is not a given, so be sure to ask; don't assume. Some accordion dealers might just do the minimum to get it into marginal working order and hope to get it out the door for more than they paid. However, if the dealer has actually refurbished it, then in the end that might be the biggest bargain of all, because you will see the exact total cost up front, rather than having to pay for unforeseen repairs after you buy.

Whether you rely on a dealer or go it on your own, you will have many decisions to make along the way about what kind of accordion you want. This guide will help inform those decisions by giving you a sound basis for comparing one accordion to another. There are many different features available in various combinations that all add up to lots and lots of options.

2.

Understanding the Options

There are many different types of piano accordions. They vary in terms of the number of bass buttons, number of treble keys, treble keyboard length, treble key width, number of treble reed sets, number of bass reed sets, treble reed configuration, basic tuning, cabinet size, overall weight, musette vs. dry tuning, tone chambers, mute chambers, reed response, keyboard action, sound quality and volume, exterior ornamentation, and physical condition. This buyer's guide explores these parameters one at a time, describes the options available, and suggests some ways to help you decide which options are best suited for you. It will also suggest some ways to evaluate quality and condition, to help you get at least a rough idea about how much repair work your accordion might need.

As you compare accordions, keep in mind that every design is a compromise. Larger accordions are likely to offer better sound and more flexibility due to their greater number of keys and buttons, wider keys, more reed sets, more switches, and better cabinet resonance, but only at the cost of greater weight. If light weight is paramount, as it is for many of us, then some combination of sacrifices in tonal quality, flexibility, and key width or number of keys will probably have to be made.

The "perfect" accordion (in all respects other than weight) would probably weigh 35 to 40 pounds. However, most of us want an accordion under 30 pounds, and many require one under 20 pounds, so we have to compromise. This guide will help you evaluate the trade-offs in order to arrive at the best compromise for you.

Some of what follows may sound technical, but it is important to understand the major differences between accordions because these differences are critical factors in determining their utility and potential market value. How can you know if the accordion you are considering is a bargain, if you don't know how it compares in features, complexity, and quality to other accordions, or if you can't estimate its potential market value or the likely cost to repair it? I will keep the technical information to a useful minimum in Chapters 1- 24. You will find more detailed and thorough technical discussions on calculating the number of reeds in your accordion, the benefits of handmade reeds and how to recognize them, and the intricacies of musette tuning in Chapters 25, 26, and 27.

I have tried to make even those chapters accessible and understandable because I believe they will lead you to a better appreciation of your accordion and a more complete understanding of the differences between accordions. That understanding will help you compare accordions, and will help you recognize which instrument is best for you, so read them if you can.

3.

Bass Buttons and Treble Keys

The numbers of bass buttons and treble keys an accordion has are among its obvious and important distinguishing characteristics. A standard full size piano accordion has 41 treble keys (24 white keys and 17 black keys) on the right side and 120 bass buttons on the left side. The lowest treble note is the F generally regarded as the F below middle C (although that is technically true only in the clarinet reed set – see Chapter 4), and the highest treble note is A, approximately 3 1/3 octaves up the chromatic scale.

Some full size accordions have extended keyboards, offering extra notes on one or both ends of the usual range. Because these additions require more reeds and valves, they make the accordion larger and heavier, while offering limited added value for most players.

Full size 41-key 120-bass accordion (Giulietti Super).

On a standard accordion, the 120 bass buttons are arranged in six vertical rows of 20 (see the diagram on page 37). The two rows nearest the bellows are buttons that play single notes. The outer four rows play chords by opening three or four note valves at a time. The third row from the bellows plays major triads, the fourth row plays minor triads, the fifth row plays dominant seventh chords (3 or 4 notes, see below), and the sixth row plays diminished seventh triads. Although there are 40 note buttons, there are only 12 different notes in the chromatic scale. Many of the buttons are duplicates placed within easy reach for playing in various keys.

For instance, there are notes and their related families of chords for Db and also for C#, which naturally are the same note and therefore use the same reeds, but have different names consistent with music theory, and different locations consistent with the button arrangement in accordance with the circle of fifths. Similarly, there are buttons for each member of the enharmonic pairs Eb and D#, Gb and F#, Ab and G#, Bb and A#. There are Fb, Cb, and even Bbb buttons, as well as their enharmonic equivalents, E, B, and A, and E#, B#, F##, and C## buttons, as well as their enharmonic equivalents, F, C, G, and D (Can you find them all on the diagram?).

Most modern accordions are designed to open only three notes when a 7th button is pushed (the root, major third, and flatted seventh). However, many older accordions have four note sevenths which also play the fifth note of the scale. The newer accordions with three note 7th chords offer more flexibility in combining chord buttons to form jazz chords. You can determine which type yours is by counting the pegs on the sides of the seventh button pistons. Four pegs engage four levers to open four note valves, while three pegs open just three valves (see the photo of bass pistons in Chapter 16).

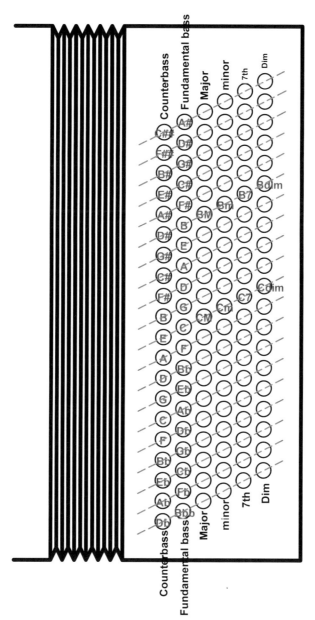

Bass button layout (120 bass)

As the preceding diagram shows, the note buttons and their related chord buttons are arranged in accordance with the circle of fifths, which basically means that no matter which button you are on, the button right above it is a perfect fifth higher, and the button right below is a perfect fourth higher. This arrangement is very convenient for most types of music.

The second row from the bellows is called the fundamental bass row because each button in that row plays the root note of the family of chords in the diagonal row of buttons adjacent to it. The row of buttons closest to the bellows is called the counter-bass row. It contains all the same notes as the fundamental bass row, but is displaced a major third upward, so that the counter-bass button diagonally down and toward the bellows from each fundamental bass button is a major third above it. Notice that this very conveniently locates all three notes of the major triad adjacent to one another (root, major third, and fifth). This arrangement of buttons in accordance with the circle of fifths is called a Stradella bass system.

Some Stradella bass accordions have 140 bass buttons, with the extra 20 buttons usually being in an extra counter-bass row located closest to the bellows. This row also contains all the same notes as the other two rows, and in the same order, but its buttons are usually displaced a minor third above the fundamental bass buttons in order to conveniently locate the minor third for playing in minor keys. Note that in this arrangement, immediately behind each fundamental bass note lies its major third, and immediately behind that lies its minor third (For a more thorough discussion of the circle of fifths, perfect fifths, perfect fourths, major thirds, minor thirds, and enharmonic pairs, consult any book on basic music theory).

I have heard that in a relatively few Stradella 140 bass accordions, the extra 20 buttons reside in a new row of augmented chord buttons located farthest from the bellows. Naturally, these accordions have just one counter-bass row.

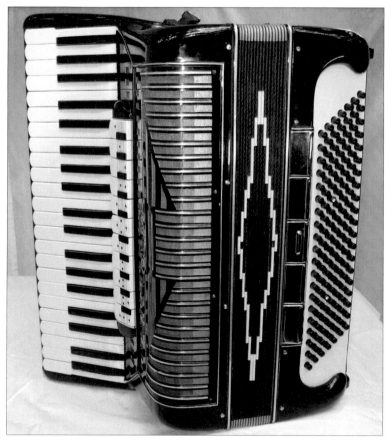

140 bass accordion. 7 vertical rows of 20 buttons.

Another less common bass system is called free bass. In the free bass system, all buttons play individual notes. Since there are no chord buttons, several buttons must be pressed simultaneously to play a chord. The free bass system allows greater flexibility in select ing any desired chord inversion, as well as in playing melodies with the left hand. It is particularly useful for playing classical music, but requires special skills possessed by relatively few accordion players.

A third option on the bass side is a converter. This allows the player to select either the standard Stradella bass system or the free bass system by pressing one of the switches.

Converter bass

Many smaller, lighter accordions have fewer treble keys and fewer bass buttons than full size standard accordions. One popular configuration is 96/37, having 96 bass buttons (6 vertical rows of 16) and 37 treble keys. The treble keyboard usually starts on the G below middle C and ends on G three octaves higher, but sometimes runs F to F. Some 96-bass accordions have 39 or some other number of treble keys. Even though these accordions have fewer bass buttons, they offer the same number of bass notes and chords. They merely have fewer repetitions (fewer enharmonic pairs) of some notes and thus less convenience in reaching some of the bass notes and chords when playing in certain keys.

Other accordions have 80 bass buttons (5 rows of 16, omitting the diminished row). Some have 72 (6 rows of 12), some have 48 (either 6 rows of 8 or 4 rows of 12), and some have even fewer, going all the way down to 12 bass buttons (2 rows of 6).

96/39 accordion (96 bass buttons, 39 keys)

12-bass accordions generally offer only two octaves on the treble side, and even some 48 bass accordions offer only one or two more notes than that. Such small accordions offer limited ability to play in all keys, a serious compromise justified only in cases where light weight and compact design outweigh all other considerations.

12-bass accordion

4.

Reed Configurations

Standard full size accordions have four sets of treble reeds and five sets of bass reeds. These are often referred to as 4/5 accordions. The five complete octaves on the bass side are played together in various octave combinations allowed by switches, but the individual notes throughout those five octaves are not separately accessible via separate bass buttons, except in free bass accordions.

Some full size accordions have five reed sets on each side and are called 5/5. Those with three sets on the treble side and five sets on the bass side are called 3/5, and so on. You may also encounter 5/6 accordions and 4/6 accordions, but the most common configurations are 4/5, 3/5, 3/4 and 2/4.

Generally, more bass reed sets produce a better bass sound and help support a higher market value, but the treble reed configuration is more interesting and is a more important determinant of value. An explanation of why this is the case requires an understanding of some basic accordion terminology.

The first terms to understand are "L", "M", and "H". "L" stands for Low pitch range, "M" stands for Middle pitch range, and "H" stands for High pitch range.

These names do not denote mutually exclusive low, middle, and high pitch ranges, as there is a lot of overlap among the sets. The L set begins at F2 in piano terminology, while the M set begins one octave higher at F3, and the H set begins one octave higher still, at Piano F4. Each set runs 41 notes up the chromatic scale, extending upward 3 1/3 octaves to A6 for the L set, to A7 for the M set, and to A8 for the H set. This arrangement of overlapping reed sets staggered at one octave intervals allows an overall pitch range of 5 1/3 octaves on a single 3 1/3 octave keyboard. It also provides the possibility (by using the master switch) of playing any note in three octaves at once by pressing just one key.

The reeds in the L set are sometimes referred to as "the bassoon reeds", those in the M set are sometimes referred to as "the clarinet reeds", and those in the H set are sometimes referred to as "the piccolo reeds".

A standard full size accordion is an "LMMH 4-reed", meaning that it has four sets of treble reeds, including one set of bassoon (L) reeds, two sets of clarinet (M) reeds, and one set of piccolo (H) reeds. Other common configurations are LMH (3-reed), LM (2-reed), and LMM (3-reed including two M sets). These are mostly found in ladies size and intermediate size accordions (see Chapter 9 for an explanation of the various accordion sizes).

Less common are LMMM (4-reed including three M sets), and LMMMH (5-reed including three M sets). See Chapter 8 for ways to identify the reed configuration of your accordion, and see

Chapter 5 for important information about the significance of multiple sets of clarinet (M) reeds.

Basic tuning can be an issue, too. Some accordions are tuned to A440, which is the modern standard for all instruments, and some are tuned to A442. A few are tuned to A441, and some old ones from the 1930s seem to be tuned to other values of A (My Piatanesi 1933 World's Fair model was tuned to A446 when I got it). If you play solo, it does not matter much, but if you play with other musicians, you might prefer an accordion tuned to A440. If this is important to you, then you should buy one with the tuning you want, as retuning an entire accordion to a different standard is very time consuming and expensive.

5.

Musette Tuning

Note that some of the configurations listed in the previous chapter include two or three sets of M reeds. Having more than one M set gives an accordion the possibility of having musette tuning. Musette tuning produces a tremolo effect caused by two reeds playing together that are just slightly out of tune with each other. Musette tuning is sometimes also called "wet" tuning. This tremolo effect is very desirable in many folk music traditions, including French musette waltzes, hence the name, "musette tuning".

The tremolo you hear is actually the "beat" caused by the two reeds coming into phase with each other several times per second. You will hear it as a subtle, rapid "wah-wah-wah-wah" fluctuation in volume. Expect to hear one or two beats (wahs) per second at the low frequency end of your keyboard and six to ten beats per second at the high end. The frequency of the beat should increase smoothly as you progress from note to note up the keyboard. If it does not, then expect to pay extra to have it properly tuned.

In LMM and LMMH musette tuned accordions, one of the

M sets is tuned to concert pitch and the other set is tuned slightly sharp or flat. One or more of the treble switches allows playing one reed from each of these two sets together in order to produce a relatively light musette sound, i.e., a relatively slow tremolo beat.

Although many LMM and LMMH accordions are tuned too wet (too fast a beat) for my taste, an even heavier musette sound (relatively faster tremolo beat) can be obtained with LMMM and LMMMH accordions, where one of the three M sets is tuned to concert pitch, one set is tuned slightly sharp, and one set is tuned slightly flat. (In some cases, instead of being tuned flat, the third set is tuned slightly sharper than the second set). Selecting various combinations of these reed sets enables varying degrees of tremolo, with the stronger tremolo effects (faster beat) being called "wetter".

To some ears, very wet tuning sounds unpleasant. However, many people like it. It is clearly a matter of personal taste.

Learn to recognize the musette sound, because particularly among 3-reed accordions, musette tuning brings a higher market value. LMM musette accordions are generally worth several hundred dollars more than otherwise similar LMH accordions.

Be aware that not all LMMH accordions are wet tuned. Some, particularly among those with tone chambers, are dry tuned. That is, they have both M sets tuned to concert pitch, but with one M set located in the tone chamber and one M set outside the tone chamber. The one in the tone chamber produces a louder, more resonant sound, and combining the two sets gives a richer, fuller tone without tremolo.

For a more thorough technical discussion of musette tuning, see Chapter 25. Tone chambers are explained in Chapter 6.

6.

Tone Chambers

Most top of the line accordions have tone chambers ("*cassotto*" is the singular form in Italian). These are resonance chambers, constructed of wood or aluminum. Reed sets mounted in tone chambers produce a richer tone. Tone chambers are most commonly found on the treble side, but sometimes also on the bass side. On the treble side, the bassoon reeds (L) and one of the clarinet sets (M1) are typically mounted in the tone chamber and the piccolo set (H) and the second clarinet set (M2) are mounted outside the chamber. This is called a double tone chamber because two sets of reeds are in the chamber. In some 3-reed LMH accordions, you may find that only the bassoon set (L) is in the chamber. This arrangement is called a single tone chamber. Accordions with tone chambers nearly always command a higher price than otherwise similar accordions without tone chambers.

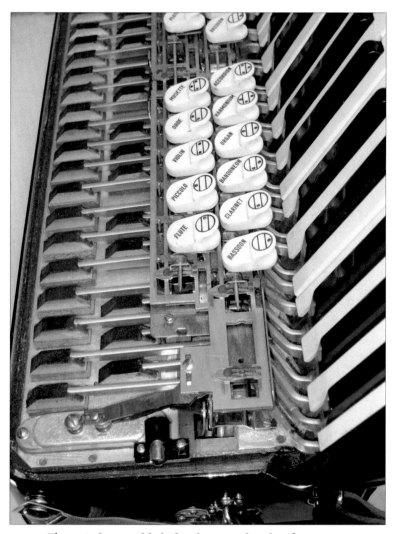

The switch assembly hides the tone chamber from view.

With switches removed, the tone chamber can be seen between the short 2-port valves and the keyboard. There is another identical set of 2-port valves down inside the tone chamber.

Accordion with no tone chamber. Note the longer valve pallets to accommodate all four ports under one valve (one port for each of the four treble reed sets).

Inside view of accordion with tone chamber.
The reeds seen face-on are in a reed block mounted to the tone
chamber, and another reed block is mounted just behind it, out of
view. The bottom two reed blocks are mounted to the foundation plate
outside the tone chamber, just as in non-tone chamber accordions.

Inside view with no tone chamber. Note that all reed blocks are
mounted to the foundation plate. Compare to the above photo of
reeds mounted to a tone chamber.

7.

Mute Chambers

Many accordions have mute chambers instead of tone chambers, and a few accordions have both. Most accordions have neither type of chamber.

Mute chambers are enclosures over the treble valves that muffle or mute the sound coming from the treble reeds. In addition to reducing the volume, they sometimes also produce a resonance similar to that of a tone chamber, without the expense of a tone chamber. However, all the reed sets are in the mute chamber, so the flexibility of selecting combinations of reed sets in and out of the chamber is lost. Mute chambers normally have switches that open their hinged doors (or more commonly, many small sliding doors), offering the option of playing with the mute chamber open for a clearer, brassier sound.

The mute chamber is hidden under this treble grille.

With the treble grille removed, you can see the wooden mute chamber, with its sliding doors open.

Now the mute chamber sliding doors are closed.

Mute chamber doors open

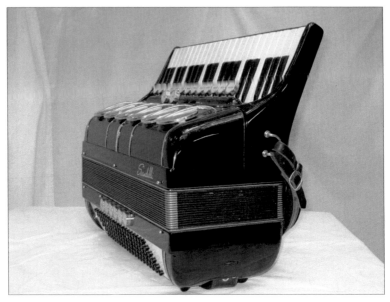

Mute chamber doors closed

8.

Number of Switches and Reeds

On most accordions there are from one to seven switches on the bass side and from one to twelve switches on the treble side. These switches operate sliding gates that block air flow to certain reed sets. Some treble and bass switches allow playing on just one of the reed sets at a time (by cutting off the air flow to the other sets), and some switches cut off air flow to only one set, allowing all the other sets to sound, while still other switches enable various combinations of reed sets. The master switch opens all the gates, bringing all reed sets on that side of the accordion into play at once.

The various available combinations allow a variety of tonal qualities, or timbres. Some accordions have enough switches to allow playing all the possible combinations, while some other accordions allow playing only on certain preferred combinations. Generally, the higher quality accordions enable more combinations, while those that might not sound so good on just one reed set sometimes don't allow selection of that reed set alone. This is seen in some 3-reed accordions that do not allow selection of just the bassoon set.

Don't be fooled by the number of switches. More switches do not necessarily mean more available reed combinations, particularly on 2-reed and 3-reed accordions. Some of these accordions have just one switchable reed set, but have one switch to turn it off and another to turn it on, thus artificially doubling the number of switches. Others have two or more switches that select the exact same reed combinations, apparently just to make the accordion appear more sophisticated. Some LMMH accordions may at first glance appear to be limited because they have just four rocker switches, but don't be fooled, because if each rocker switch controls one of the four reed sets, as was common on some older Excelsior accordions, then various combinations of these four switches can enable as many useful reed combinations as accordions having fifteen switches. The number of switches can be misleading.

Far more important are the number of reed sets in the accordion and the number of different reed combinations that can be selected via switches. On an LMMH accordion, there are fifteen theoretically possible combinations of reed sets: L, M1, M2, H, LM1, LM2, LH, MM, M1H, M2H, LM1H, LM2H, LMM, MMH, and LMMH (master). However, very few accordions allow LM2, LM2H, and M2H, leaving only twelve common combinations.

On LMM musette accordions there are only five useful combinations: L, LM1, M1, MM, and LMM. Note that M2 is used only along with M1 (never alone) because it is out of tune with other instruments. On LMH accordions there are seven potentially useful combinations: L, M, H, LM, LH, MH, and LMH. Check to see how many of the potential combinations can actually be selected.

A common and appealing method of labeling switches uses symbols based on a circle divided into three horizontal bands. A dot in the bottom band means L, a dot in the middle band means M, and a dot in the top band means H. Thus, a symbol with two dots in the middle band is used on the switch that selects the MM combination, and a symbol with one dot in each of the top and bottom bands and two dots in the middle band is used on the master switch of LMMH accordions. With this labeling system, one can deduce an accordion's reed configuration by just looking at the switch labels. Add up all the dot positions to get the number of reeds. The one below is an LMMH. The master switch is elsewhere.

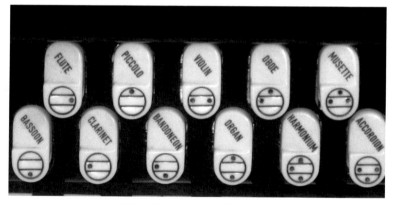

Unambiguous switch labels

Unfortunately, there are also many other more ambiguous switch labeling systems, using fanciful names like violin, flute, celeste, oboe, harmonium, accordion, organ, etc., without any diagrams or other clarification.

Ambiguous switch labels.

In some cases, the switches don't have any labels at all, leaving you to discover and remember where the various timbres are to be found. In these cases, the reed configuration can best be ascertained by trying all the switches and listening very carefully to determine which reed sets are selected by each switch. Alternatively, you can look inside the accordion to see what reeds it contains. (See chapter 15 for how to open the accordion.)

Once you have the accordion open, you can identify the reed sets and therefore the accordion's reed configuration by looking at the size of the reeds, checking for weights on the tips of the reed tongues, and by seeing how many of the reeds in each set have reed valves (leathers or plastic *ventilli*).

You can identify a bassoon reed set by finding the two rows that contain the largest reeds (lowest notes) and which have weights added to the tips of the reed tongues on the three or four lowest notes in each row. These are always the bassoon set. Also, all the reeds in any bassoon set have reed valves, whereas this is not true of any other set.

One row of the bassoon reed set

You can identify the clarinet set (or sets) by finding the rows with the next smaller reeds, and with the last four or five reeds at the smallest end of each row not having reed valves.

One row of clarinet reeds. No leathers on the last four.

You may find one, two, or three complete clarinet reed sets. Each set will normally be split into two rows. One row of each set primarily contains the black key notes for that set and the other row contains all or most of the white key notes for that set.

For example, an LMMMH accordion would have six rows of clarinet reeds comprising three complete M sets. Naturally, it would also have two rows of bassoon reeds (one full set) and two rows of piccolo reeds (one full set). With ten rows of reeds in five reed blocks, it is no wonder that LMMMH accordions are a bit heavier than other configurations.

Similarly, an LMMH or any other 4-reed accordion normally has eight rows of reeds in four reed blocks, while 3-reed accordions usually have six rows of reeds in three reed blocks.

In some designs, the reed blocks are short and mounted transversely, rather than longitudinally, in which case there are more of them and each reed set is broken up among all the reed blocks, making it difficult to identify the reed configuration with just a quick look inside the accordion.

You can identify a piccolo reed set by finding the two rows with very tiny reeds at one end, with the ten smallest reeds in each row not having reed valves. Note that not all accordions have piccolo reeds, for example, LM, MM, LMM, and LMMM accordions do not have any piccolo reeds.

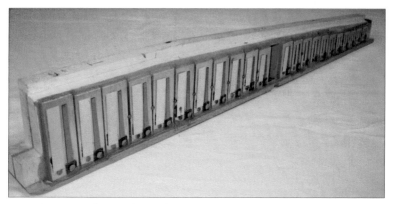

One row of piccolo reeds. No leathers on the last ten reeds.

One quick way to identify how many treble reed sets an accordion has is to count the ports under the treble valves. In an accordion with no tone chamber, all available reed sets are controlled by a single set of valves, so that a 2-reed accordion has two ports under each valve, a 3-reed has three, and so on. To find out how many reed sets your accordion has, remove the treble grille, press any key, peek under the valve that lifts, and count the ports. The accordion contains one reed set for each port. In tone chamber accordions, one or two (usually two) of the reed sets are in the tone chamber and are controlled by a separate set of valves that are much harder to peek under, because they are located down inside the tone chamber, so in this case it is better to look inside the accordion.

**Valve removed to allow counting ports (and reed sets, since this
3-reed accordion obviously has no tone chamber).**

In some cases, the master switch is located with all the other switches,
but in many cases, it is a long bar along the edge of the keyboard, called a
palm master. Some accordions have both types of master switch.

Palm master switch.

Regardless of its location, the master switch turns on (opens the gates to) all reed sets. Some accordions also have chin switches, which are buttons on the top of the accordion that can be pressed with the chin to allow changing registers without taking the hand off the keyboard.

View from the inside of the bellows, with treble reed blocks removed and all switch slides open (master switch on), leaving the leather treble valve surfaces visible through the ports.

All switch slides are closed, cutting off air to the valves (For illustration purposes only, as there is not normally a switch that does this, except on electronic accordions).

9.

Size

People and hands come in all sizes. Different sized people need different sized accordions. Fortunately, many different sizes of accordions are available. Standard full-size (4/5 LMMH 120/41) accordions have approximately 19-inch keyboards, varying up to 19 1/2-inch on some models (keyboards are measured from the top of the top white key to the bottom of the bottom white key). These keyboards provide keys wide enough for nearly everyone's fingers. However, the octave reach on these accordions is longer than on so-called "ladies'-size" accordions, and thumb-under arpeggios can be a difficult reach for people with small hands.

Ladies'-size 120/41 LMM and LMH accordions generally have keyboard lengths in the range of 15½ inches to 17½ inches, and thus have narrower keys and a shorter octave reach. The narrower keys, especially on the 15 to 16 inch keyboards, make these accordions difficult to play for people with large hands and fingers.

Before buying any accordion, you should make sure the

keyboard and keys are the right size for your hand and fingers. If you find yourself hitting two notes when you meant to play one, then you might need an accordion with wider keys. If you find the octave reach a real stretch, then you might prefer narrower keys.

By the way, don't be fooled by the name. Many women play full-size accordions and many men play ladies'-size. It's all a matter of finding the accordion that is the right size for your body and is comfortable to play.

Accordions with keyboards between 17 ½ and 19 inches long are sometimes called "intermediate" size. Some really old accordions (1930's and earlier) have 20-inch keyboards, making their keys even wider than the current standard. Many 37 key accordions have full standard width keys, yet have shorter keyboards due to the smaller number of keys.

Another size consideration is your height. If you find the accordion too high up under your chin (or if you can't even see over it) while playing sitting down, then you probably need a smaller accordion. You may also want a smaller accordion if you will be traveling with it. Most ladies' size accordions will fit in most airline overhead baggage compartments, but full size accordions will often not fit. Since checking an accordion as baggage is very risky for the accordion, you should use a smaller model when traveling so you can carry it on board.

Ladies'-size and full-size, side by side. Both have 41 treble keys and 120 bass buttons.

10.

Weight

Smaller accordions tend to weigh less, so you might want a smaller accordion just for its lighter weight, especially if you play standing up. Standard full-size 4/5 accordions usually weigh between 22 and 28 pounds, while ladies'-size 3/4 accordions generally weigh between 16 and 20 pounds. The weight difference can be significant if you play standing or strolling for long periods. If you always sit down to play, the accordion rests on your lap, making instrument weight much less of an issue.

Naturally, 2-reed accordions tend to be lighter than 3-reed accordions, which in turn tend to be lighter than 4-reed accordions. However, this is not always the case, so you should actually compare the weights.

The really old accordions tend to be lighter than more recent models. However, the later models were made heavier for good reason. Some of the older ones were so light and flimsy that they did not hold up well, and tended to warp and flex, sometimes causing air leaks around the valves that are difficult to seal.

The really old ones (prior to 1940) also have very deep key action and nearly square edges on the keys, making them difficult to play. They require extensive keyboard modifications to make them easier to play and to give them a more modern feel. Nevertheless, once these modifications are made, playing one of these antiques can be very satisfying for people who appreciate old instruments, and they offer the additional advantage of lighter weight.

When comparing accordion weights, be sure to understand whether strap weight is being included. A standard set of wide padded shoulder straps weighs about 1 1/4 pounds and can skew your comparisons. Finally, notice that balance can be as important as weight. An accordion that hangs comfortably can feel lighter and actually be less of a strain on your back than a lighter one that does not feel so well balanced. The bottom line is that rather than just weighing it, you have to try the accordion on and play it standing up for a while to see how heavy it feels compared to others.

We all want an accordion that weighs under 15 pounds, but we have to compromise in order to get other features we want. 12-bass accordions weigh under 15 pounds, but offer limited utility. Some 48 to 96 bass accordions now being manufactured (mostly 2-reed) fall within or close to that weight limit, but offer limited switching options, smaller keyboards (fewer keys), and unknown durability. Some people like the sound they produce, and some don't. If light weight is important to you, then one of these accordions might be the right choice.

Light weight always comes at a price. Lighter cabinet construction using lighter and thinner wood impacts tonal qualities, rigidity, and durability. Fewer buttons, keys, and reed sets adversely impact flexibility in the type of music you can play, as well as the tonal options available. Narrower keys can make it difficult for people with wide fingers to play. Designers of the smallest accordions generally tune them very wet to get more sound out of a smaller box. Although they may sound bright and cheery, this excessively wet tuning can eventually get on your nerves.

Every design is a compromise. Finding the right compromise for you is a very personal decision. This guide will help you understand the options and trade-offs available, to enable you to make the right decision.

11.

Reed Quality

Reeds are the heart of any accordion, and "handmade reeds" ("*voci a mano*" in Italian) are the hallmark of the very best accordions. They generally respond better at lower bellows pressure (playing softly), tolerate higher pressures (louder volume) with less frequency distortion, and produce a better, fuller sound. However, handmade reeds are relatively expensive, and accordions with handmade reeds command significantly higher prices.

There is much confusion about handmade reeds. Some people think they may not really be handmade at all, that the name is just a label used to denote the higher manufacturing standards applied to the highest quality reeds. Some feel that since today's handmade reeds are partly made by machine, they are therefore not really handmade in the old tradition, and should be called hand fitted. Some people point out that handmade reeds are not necessarily any better than other reeds because the quality obviously depends on the skill of the hands that make them.

Many accordion players do not hear or feel a significant

difference between some handmade reeds and the next grade down (hand fitted reeds, or *"voci tipo a mano"* in Italian). Some even say the best hand fitted reeds might even be better than some handmade reeds, and this is probably true.

However, in some cases the difference is undeniable. The reed response on the accordion I tried out at the Beltuna factory in Castelfidardo was astounding. It was unequivocally better than on any other accordion I have ever played, including my Giulietti Super, which also has handmade reeds.

The lesson here is that quality varies, even among handmade reeds. To evaluate the quality and condition of any accordion, you must play it and compare it to other accordions. You cannot rely on unsupported claims of high quality, and you cannot infer superior quality solely from brand names or from claims that an accordion has handmade reeds.

To evaluate the reeds, check for response at very low bellows pressure and for frequency stability at very high bellows pressure. The lowest notes in the bassoon set are the most sensitive to both of these tests. Squeeze or pull the bellows very gently and see if the note will play. The softer you can play these notes and the less air they use, the better the quality.

Also see how loudly the reeds will play without going flat. Better frequency stability at higher bellows pressure indicates better quality reeds. This may be due to the harder duraluminum reed plate allowing a tighter rivet connection between the reed tongue and the reed plate.

Test several reeds, though, because reed response is also highly dependent on reed voicing (the adjustment of the elevation of the tip of the reed tongue above the plane of the reed plate), as well as on the condition of the leathers. If some of the lowest frequency reeds seem highly responsive and some don't, it could be because some of them are not properly voiced or because their leathers are bad. If any of them choke (refuse to sound or delay sounding under sudden high bellows pressure), they will need to be properly voiced before you can meaningfully test them.

The advantages of handmade reeds are most apparent at the low end of the keyboard because it is here that machine made reeds reveal their greatest weaknesses. The lowest notes emanate from the largest reeds, which have greater mass, requiring more air to get them moving. Due to their larger size, they also have a greater distance around the perimeter of the reed tongue, and thus more space for air to leak between the reed tongue and the vent rather than driving it. These two factors, 1) more air required to drive the reed and 2) less of the available air being put to work driving it, compound to make the lowest note reeds the least responsive on our keyboards. That's why you need more bellows pressure to play the lowest notes in the bassoon reed set. It is here that handmade reeds are most needed and where they have the greatest advantage.

Comparing a Binci handmade reed to a machine made reed at the lowest F in the bassoon reed set reveals striking differences in thickness and contour that allow the Binci reed to be lighter than the machine made reed. The machine made reed is of nearly uniform thickness along its length, while the Binci reed is very thin near the fixed end and steps up in thickness twice as we approach the free end. This design puts the center of gravity closer to the tip than it would be on a similar length reed tongue of nearly constant thickness, thus allowing the Binci reed to be significantly thinner throughout most of its length, and therefore lighter, while still vibrating at the assigned frequency.

The clearance between the reed tongue and the vent is smaller on the Binci reed, reducing the air loss around the tongue and putting more of the available air to work driving the reed. Perhaps due to its lower mass, as well as to less leakage, the Binci reed is also properly voiced using a noticeably smaller elevation of the tip of the reed tongue above the reed plate. This probably further reduces the air loss around the reed tongue, thereby helping to make the Binci reed more responsive.

I also compared the Binci handmade reeds to the handmade reeds in my Giulietti Super, and the Binci reed appears to have advantages, primarily in lighter weight, lending further credence to the notion that not all handmade reeds are equal. While it is probably true that some hand fitted reeds are better than some handmade reeds, I doubt that there are hand fitted reeds that can match the responsiveness of the Binci handmade reeds. If there are, I would like to see them.

For a more complete explanation of how handmade reeds can be so much better, and very clear instructions on how to recognize them, supported by close-up color photographs comparing handmade reeds to machine made reeds, see the technical discussion in Chapter 26.

12.

Keyboard Action

Piano accordion keyboards vary greatly in the feel of the keyboard action. Some are deep, some shallow. Some are stiff, some light and easy. Some keys have very rounded edges, making glissando easier, while some have rather blunt edges. Some rebound quickly, others seem slow. Some of these differences are due to age, wear, corrosion, and dirt. The following information is included to help you understand what repairs your accordion keyboard might need in order to bring it into good condition or to modify it to your liking.

The standard depth of key travel since the 1960s seems to be around 1/4 inch. Older accordions typically have deeper action, sometimes approaching 1/2 inch. Some owners of these accordions have their keyboards modified for shallower action, usually around 3/16 inch travel, but sometimes as little as 1/8 inch, which is pushing the limit. If you set it too shallow, some of the valves may not open far enough to clearly sound all the reeds.

This is especially true among extended keyboard accordions and ladies'-size 120/41 accordions in which space constraints force designers to put two or three of the white key reeds in the black key reed block, which also puts their valve pallets in the row with the black key valves, i.e., the row closer to the keyboard. Having their valves closer to the keyboard gives these keys shorter lever arms, and therefore less valve lift for a given amount of key travel. Less valve lift allows less air to pass through the reeds behind those valves.

Some designers employ compound levers to equalize the valve travel of these notes, but if your accordion's designer did not, then setting these keys too low (to get a very shallow key action) can cause these valves not to open far enough to sound all the reeds, especially the bassoon reeds, which require the most air. Check for compound levers on those two or three notes in order to know if your keyboard can be set up for white key travel shallower than 3/16".

Some progressive deepening of key travel occurs naturally with age and use as the felt pads under the keys compress, as the leather treble valve facings seat into their ports, and as the felt padding under that leather compresses with age. The effects of these latter two processes can be seen directly by removing the treble grille, depressing a key, and looking at the bottom of the valve as it lifts off its seat. The depth of the waffle pattern of the ports imprinted in the bottom of the valve is a direct indication of this settling. Flattening of the nap on the leather is normal, even on new accordions, but if you can see any bulging in the waffle pattern, it is an indication of compression of the felt under the leather. Sometimes you will notice that moth larvae have damaged the felt, causing it to collapse, in which case it is definitely time for new valves.

Naturally, as the valve settles against its seat due to these causes, the key on the opposite side of the fulcrum (key hinge and spindle) elevates, thus deepening the action. The effects of this can be seen by looking down the edge of the keyboard. Any differences in height among the keys indicate that some valves have settled more than others. Any keys sitting higher than the ends of the keyboard cabinet are probably the result of this settling, as the accordion almost certainly left the factory with all white keys exactly level with the ends of the cabinet. Sometimes a key is bent way out of alignment by catching a finger or a strap under it or by catching it on the edge of the case while putting the accordion into its case. However, the differential settling I'm describing here causes a more subtle misalignment, usually less than 1/16 inch.

The visual and tactile effects of this settling (as well as more severe misalignment) can be reversed by leveling the keyboard. Leveling the keyboard involves bending the key rods to set the correct key height, while also maintaining a perfect air tight seal at the valve. Note that leveling does not reverse the compression of the felt, it merely makes the keyboard look and feel better.

During the keyboard leveling process, the keys can be set even lower than the original factory setting in order to create a shallower action than originally intended by the designer. Another way to make the action shallower is to install thicker than original felt pads under all the keys to restrict their downward travel.

Be aware that if the old felt under the leather valve facings is compressed, it is probably also less resilient, contributing to a noisier keyboard. When the key is released, the key spring slams the valve shut. One of the purposes of the felt padding under the valve face is to help absorb this impact in order to reduce noise. Many older accordions have very noisy keyboards partly because the felt valve padding has deteriorated or compressed.

The problem can be at least partially mitigated by installing new felt and leather valve facings. It can be further mitigated by setting a shallower than original key action, because reducing the amount of travel also reduces the time the spring has in which to accelerate the key, which in turn reduces the maximum velocity and momentum of the key. Reducing the momentum also reduces the objectionable clatter as the valve slams shut. The combination of fresh felt and a shallower action can make the keyboard significantly quieter.

One of the most noticeable differences between keyboards is the amount of finger pressure required to depress a key. Some accordions have very strong key springs, making the keys relatively hard to press. This extra spring pressure helps maintain a better air seal at the treble valves, but can make the accordion hard to play. This was the case with my Lo Duca when I first got it, so I removed all the keys and springs, and reshaped all the springs to fit a new template (so all keys would offer equal resistance). You might want to do the same if your new accordion seems too hard to play.

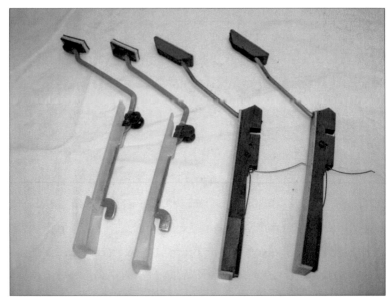

Typical treble keys, two with springs

I recently repaired an accordion that had different spring pressure on different keys. Investigation revealed that some of the key springs were misaligned, so they were offering less than normal resistance. The keys had to be removed to allow proper alignment of the springs. If your new accordion has this problem, you should plan on disassembling the keyboard and properly installing (or possibly replacing) some of the key springs.

The final consideration on keyboard feel is the edges of the keys, especially in very old accordions (1930s and older). Making the action shallower will help make glissandos easier, but if your key edges are square or only slightly beveled, glissandos will still be difficult.

The solution may be to bevel the edges of all the white keys. This is time consuming, but if done correctly, it can leave the keys looking as if they had originally been made that way.

The main point is that if you are buying a used accordion with a keyboard that seems a bit clunky, you might want to budget some money to renew the valves, make the action shallower, level the keyboard, and quiet it down. The keyboard can probably be restored and upgraded to your liking for a few hundred dollars.

13.

Exterior Ornamentation

Accordion cabinets are made of wood, but usually have a celluloid exterior finish available in bright colors, as well as black and some multicolor layouts. In addition, some are elaborately decorated with rhinestones (sometimes colored rhinestones in elaborate patterns on painted backgrounds, such as gold rhinestones on a gold background or blue rhinestones on a blue background). My Piatanesi 1933 World's Fair Model has an iridescent finish that changes from gold to red to green as you view it from different angles, and over 900 rhinestones.

Many people like ornate accordions, which tends to drive the price up. If you want a fancy one, you will probably have to pay a little more.

Ornate accordion detail

14.

Air Leaks

Air tightness is a major consideration. Most old accordions leak air somewhere, either through screw holes or cracks in the cabinet, or between the cabinet and the foundation plate, or through one of the bellows gaskets, or around one or more of the 41 treble valves and 24 bass valves, or through the switch linkage, or through the bellows themselves. Sometimes missing or broken reeds cause significant air leaks. Loose reed blocks can also waste a lot of air. Bad leathers can also increase air consumption. There are lots of possible sources of leaks, and a few small leaks can add up to a significant loss of air and accordion performance. Air leakage can make an accordion difficult to play.

You should compare the "bellows tightness" of any prospective purchase to that of other accordions. If the one you are considering seems to use more air than others, it probably needs repair. If you don't know how it should feel, then have an experienced player try it.

No one wants to play an air hog. That's what I call an accordion that requires too much bellows pumping to play. If the bellows reaches the end of its travel before you get to the end of a musical phrase or two, then it has too many air leaks to be useful. If you are considering buying an accordion that uses too much air, then you will want to understand the nature of the problem before deciding how much to pay.

Sometimes air leaks are obvious, as when you can feel a blast of air hitting your face as you close the bellows. These obvious leaks are often simple to repair. Many other kinds of leaks are insidious sneak-thieves of your bellows air, difficult to find, and time consuming to fix, and are often a combination of several small leaks that add up to a lot of air loss. This chapter will help you find the leaks and understand what repairs might be required to fix them. You won't want to miss out on buying a good used accordion if the solution to its problem is obvious, simple, and inexpensive.

Leaks come in two categories, external and internal. External leaks are those that allow the bellows to fall open or closed without any keys or buttons being pressed. Internal leaks are those that allow air to find its way to an open note valve without first having to pass through the reed that is being played. It is important to identify whether your leaks are external or internal so some judgment can be made of the difficulty and cost of repair.

External leaks are little holes and gaps where air passes into or out of the accordion without first having to pass through the reeds and valves. Fortunately, these are the easiest to find, as the escaping air can usually be heard and felt. The most common places to find external leaks are at the bellows gaskets, around loose or missing screws, shoulder strap brackets, or switch linkages, through damaged or misaligned treble and bass valves, and through loose or missing bellows corners.

Bellows gaskets are easy to change, and loose screws can easily be tightened. Small holes in the wood can be quickly sealed with reed wax. Leaking valves can be simple and inexpensive to repair, but in some cases can be time consuming and costly, especially for leaking bass valves because they are so hard to access. A single leaking bellows corner can be easy to fix, but if more than a couple of corners are leaking, you may need a new bellows, which will be a costly repair.

Internal leaks only show themselves while a valve is open, that is, while the accordion is being played. The bellows can seem nice and tight while no keys are depressed, but the accordion consumes too much air when you play it. Sometimes these leaks can be heard as a hissing sound while a note is sounding, but their air streams can never be felt, as they are inside the accordion. The most common causes of internal leaks are bad or missing leathers, bent or broken reed tongues, loose reed plates, and loose or warped reed blocks. Internal leaks are often more time consuming to locate and repair.

To find out if your leak is internal or external, measure the amount of time it takes the bellows to close under its own weight from the full open position with all valves closed. Rest your accordion on its feet on a sturdy table. Unsnap the bellows straps, grip one end of the treble keyboard in each hand, press a few keys on each end, and lift the treble section to expand the bellows. Don't mind the discordant sound as air rushes into the bellows through the random combination of open valves. Keep lifting until the bellows is all the way open and the bass section lifts off the table. Shake it a bit to make sure the bellows is fully extended, then release all the keys so all valves are closed (but don't drop the accordion). Note the time on a clock with a sweep second hand and let the bellows close by itself under the full weight of the treble section. Don't let go, but don't hold any weight, either. Use your hands to keep the bellows going down straight, but not to hold it open or force it closed. If the bellows takes less than 30 seconds to close, it has some external leaks, as nearly all accordions do. If it takes less than 20 seconds to close, then you probably have an external air leak large enough to locate and repair.

To find the source of the leak, expand the bellows exactly as before, but this time as the bellows slowly closes under its own weight, pass your face around the exterior, feeling for drafts of air on your cheeks. Turn the accordion around and repeat the process until you have passed your face around the entire perimeter of both bellows gaskets. The skin on your face is very sensitive to tiny drafts, and most external leaks of any consequence can be found in this manner. To verify that you have found the exact source of the leak, put a small piece of masking tape over the suspected source and repeat the test. If the leak can no longer be felt, then you can be pretty sure it is under the tape.

If no leaks are found around the bellows, remove the treble grille and repeat the process to check for leaks around the treble valves. You can often isolate a single leaking valve by pressing it down lightly with your finger. If this stops the leak, you have found the source. You may be able to see that this valve does not rest flat on the foundation plate, or that it is not centered over its ports. If it appears to be centered, then the leak may be due to it being slightly tipped one way or another. You can use a narrow strip of paper as a feeler gauge to feel under the edges of the valve to be sure that each end and each side of the valve is closing tightly against the foundation plate.

Another way to find treble valve leaks is to open the accordion (see Chapter 15), remove the treble reed blocks, make sure all the switch slides are open (reference the last two photos in Chapter 8), and in a dark room pass a bright light around the reed block side of the foundation plate while you look for glowing felt pads on the valve side of the plate. Any glowing felt represents a probable air leak.

Be aware, though, that on some accordions, mostly the very old ones from the 1930s and earlier, removing the reed blocks allows the foundation plate to flex, which can give false positives on this test. That is, the valves that appear to be leaking under the bright light may not actually leak when the reed blocks are re-installed and the foundation plate is once again stiffened by their presence. However, on most newer accordions, this test works very well.

This same test can be performed on the bass valves, but the bass machine must first be removed, and in the vast majority of accordions, this requires disassembling it piece by piece, a very time consuming project.

An easier way to check bass valves for leaks (especially if the leather valve facings are white) is to remove the bass reed blocks and look at the valves from the inside. Gently press each valve open with a pencil eraser or other small blunt tool, and look for dust trails around the edges of the leather. The edges of the valves, where the nap of the leather has been flattened by contact with the foundation plate, should be clean. Dirty looking leather along these edges is an indication of a chronic air leak. You may also find some tiny wood shavings, wax chips, or other foreign matter lodged under the valve, preventing it from sealing against the foundation plate, in which case you can probably cure the problem by removing the obstruction with a pair of tweezers.

Wood splinter under bass valve.

Sometimes, many individually imperceptible leaks in the bellows can add up to a significant external air leak. In this case, the only remedy is a new bellows, which at this writing, runs around $350. However, this is fairly unusual, so eliminate all the other possible leak sources before committing to a new bellows.

If your timed bellows collapse test reveals no significant external air leaks, but the accordion uses too much air when you play it, then you probably have an internal leak. To evaluate those, you will need to open the accordion (see Chapter 15).

When you have it open, check first for bad leathers and broken, loose, or missing reeds. There may be some problems that you can't see, that will show up only on a test bellows, but don't worry about that right now, just look for obvious problems. If lots of leathers are curled back from their reed plates, you may have to spend up to a few hundred dollars to have new leathers installed. If one or more reeds are loose or have fallen out, this may be an indication that the reed wax is brittle, and you should inspect it more carefully before buying, as re-waxing an entire accordion is an expensive repair (often over $1,000).

Also check for loose reed blocks. If they move at all when you try to wiggle them, they are too loose, and simply tightening their mounting clamp screws and/or installing a thin shim under the reed block restraint at the opposite end could cure the problem.

If you find no obvious problem, then diagnosing and repairing the internal air leak could take some time and cost some money. There may be warped reed blocks allowing air to pass under their edges and directly to the open valve ports without first passing through the desired reeds. There might be reeds deformed by excessive pressure during tuning, or reeds that need to be properly voiced.

Air might be leaking through cracks in the reed wax or around reed plates that have separated from the wax but have not yet fallen out. I have even found concealed internal defects in the reed blocks that allow air to leak between adjacent reed chambers.

The point is that in the absence of an obvious problem like bad leathers, missing reeds, or loose reed blocks, internal air leak diagnosis and repair can be time consuming and costly.

15.

Opening the Accordion

It is best to remove the shoulder straps and the back pad (if any) before opening the accordion. Once that is done, locate and count the bellows pins on the treble side of the bellows. There will usually be three on the back and three or four on the front, but there may also be one on the top and one on the bottom. Avoid marring the pins or the plastic finish on the accordion when you pull the pins. If you don't have the special pliers made for this purpose, you can wrap the jaws of any pliers with tape to pad them.

Stand the accordion on its feet, that is, with the bass plate and bass strap down. Grip each treble side bellows pin with the pliers and pull it straight out, steadying the accordion with your other hand as you do so. Some accordions have screws in place of the pins, in which case you will spin them out with a screwdriver. Keep the pins in order, as they are often not all exactly the same length or diameter, and they should be put back into the same holes they came from. (To keep them in order, I stab them into a styrofoam block in the same order in which they are to be reinstalled, front pins in the front of the block, rear pins in the rear.)

When you have removed all the pins from the treble side of the bellows, try lifting one corner of the treble section off the bellows. You may have to hold the bellows down while you pull up on the treble section. If you meet significant resistance, check for any bellows strap or snap mounting screws within a half inch of the bellows that might be penetrating the bellows frame and remove them also. Forcing the accordion apart while any screw or pin still penetrates the bellows frame will damage the bellows frame, necessitating a costly repair.

When the treble section first separates from the bellows, peek inside to see if any internal microphone wires must be disconnected before you lift it far enough to tear those wires loose from their mounting, which is often very fragile. These wires, if any, will be at the bottom (high note end) of the accordion. Once the wires are unplugged, turn the treble section over and set it on the table with the reed blocks facing upward. Now you can inspect for bad leathers, cracked wax, missing reeds, loose reed blocks, etc.

For better access to the bass reed blocks, remove the bellows from the bass section as well, but not before noting how it goes back together. If there are four bellows pins on the front of the bass section and three on the back, then it will be obvious which way the bellows goes back on. If it is not obvious, then mark the bellows frame with a pencil so you can be sure to put it back in the correct orientation, or the bellows frame will not seal and your bellows pins will not line up. Be sure to unplug any microphone wires before lifting the bellows too far.

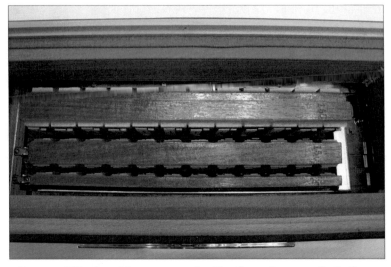

Bass reed blocks with some marginal leathers. Remove the bellows for better access.

If you are removing reed blocks, be very careful not to bend the register slides. In many older accordions, the slides are mounted in the reed block rather than in the foundation plate. If this is the case, lifting the reed block without first disengaging the slide from the switch mechanism can cause the slide to kink, rendering it useless. Once bent, they are very difficult to straighten well enough to work properly.

Note the orientation of the reed blocks and the details of the slide's connection to the linkage so you will be able to put it back exactly the way it came out, with any slides properly engaged with their control linkage. When reinstalling any reed block, make sure it is securely and rigidly fastened down so no air can leak under it.

When you have finished your interior inspection, set the bellows back onto the bass section (being careful not to catch and bend any bass reed leathers in the process), reconnecting any microphone wires as you go, and install the bass side bellows pins. Then set the treble section in place on the bellows, reconnecting any microphone wires as you go and making sure you have the bass buttons and treble keys all facing forward.

Install the bellows pins in their proper holes. If the pins are hard to push in, you can save wear and tear on your fingers by pushing them in with a small block of wood. However, if you have to push very hard, you may have the wrong pin in the wrong hole, or something misaligned. Make sure you have the best fit for all pins before forcing any pin into any hole. Finally, reinstall any bellows strap screws you may have removed, and put on the shoulder straps and back pad.

16.

Likely Repairs

The most likely repair to be needed is replacement of leathers. These are the little leather check valves glued to the reed plate on the opposite side from each reed tongue. They block the air flow through the reed tongue that is not being used, depending on the direction the air is moving. A standard 120/41 accordion usually contains around 420 leathers, and at this writing, I charge $1.50 each to change them, so if very many of them are bad, the repair cost can be significant.

Can you spot the curled leathers and the missing reeds?

The problem is that with exposure to moisture and temperature changes over time, the leathers tend to dry, harden, and curl back from the reed plate. Every leather should be soft and pliable, and should lie flat against the reed plate. Leathers that harden and/or curl back from the reed plate can cause several problems, including being noisy as they slam closed, causing a change in pitch as they close, allowing significant air leakage through the reed that is not sounding, throwing both reeds on that reed plate significantly out of tune, and sometimes preventing the reed from sounding at all. Most "tuning" problems are actually leather problems.

Nearly every old accordion needs some leathers changed, and many need most or all of them changed. Those accordions you see on eBay, being sold by people who admit knowing nothing about accordions, will almost certainly need most or all of their leathers changed. Unless you see clear photographic evidence that the leathers are in good condition, *and* unless the seller demonstrates a useful knowledge of accordions by unequivocally declaring, "every leather is soft and supple, and lies perfectly flat", you should assume that accordion will need expensive repairs.

Bad leathers curl back from the reed plate.

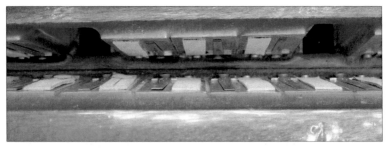

Good leathers lie flat against the reed plate.

Marginal leathers curl slightly away from the reed plate.

**Treble reed blocks with some marginal leathers, but mostly good.
Note that the smaller reeds near the right ends of clarinet and piccolo
rows do not normally have leathers.**

Keep in mind that these photos show only the outsides of the
reed blocks. There are an equal number of leathers hidden from
view inside the reed blocks, which must also be checked.

Another common problem is silent reeds. Any tiny piece of lint can lodge between a reed tongue and its reed plate, preventing the reed from vibrating. Sometimes the cure is simply to play that note loudly in order to blow out the lint. Sometimes the reed can be freed up by plucking it until it can be heard to vibrate freely. At worst, the lint can always be removed by passing a .002" or thinner metal feeler gauge between the reed tongue and the reed vent.

Reeds can also go silent due to bad leathers, or broken reed tongues, or cracked wax (which allows air to leak out around the reed plate, rather than passing over the reed). The reed plate may even have fallen out and be rattling around inside the accordion, producing a huge air leak whenever the corresponding key or button is pressed, and possibly even damaging the bellows if the accordion is played with the loose reed lodged in one of the folds.

If reeds have fallen out, the reed wax is probably brittle with age. If so, then the accordion needs new wax and leathers. Unfortunately, re-waxing and re-leathering a 120/41 LMMH accordion is about a 40 hour job, and could take longer if significant tuning is required. Apply the hourly labor rate of your local accordion repair shop to see how expensive this will be. Even at the very low shop rate of $35 per hour, this would amount to $1400 for labor alone.

Naturally, the cost would be lower for accordions with fewer keys and/or fewer reed sets, and would be higher for accordions with more keys and/or more reed sets. The point to keep in mind is that if the wax has gone bad, the cost of repair might exceed the potential market value of the instrument.

Other common repairs include freeing treble keys and bass

buttons that stick down when you press them. Often, this is an intermittent problem, in which case you may need to play it for awhile to be sure none are sticking.

On the treble side, sticking keys are usually caused by high friction at the key hinge, which in turn is caused either by corrosion or by the oil that some misguided soul put on the hinges. Lint and dust mix with oil, eventually turning it into a sticky gunk that can gum up the key hinges. The solution is to remove the offending keys (or better yet, all the keys) and clean the key hinges and axles. Other common causes include misalignment of the key, causing it to rub on its lateral guides, a defective key spring, or interference between the key and the treble grille or switching mechanism. The bottom line is that if your potential purchase has any sticking keys, you will need to budget some repair time to fix it.

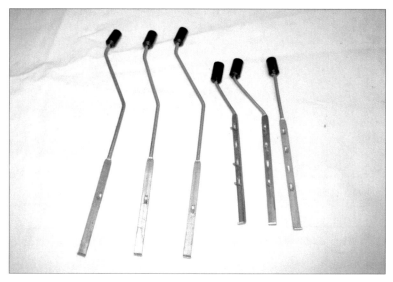

Bass buttons/pistons.

On the bass side, the most common cause of sticking buttons is high friction between the piston and the slot in the wooden guide at the bottom of it, with the root causes usually being dust and lint or corrosion. The solution in these cases is usually to remove the piston and clean it and its slot in the wooden guide. The next most common cause is one of the bell crank levers pressing against the side of the piston, causing excess friction. This can easily be cured by bending the lever away (but not so far away that it no longer engages its peg on the side of the piston). However, sticking buttons can have other causes, and disassembling a bass machine to get the buttons out for cleaning or other repair can be very time consuming. Disassembling and reassembling a bass machine can take half a day or more.

Stradella bass machine

You may also encounter accordions with one or more treble keys lifted out of the keyboard at some crazy angle because someone caught a strap under it while lifting the accordion by its straps.

Usually, this is easy to fix, but in extreme cases it can cause a stress crack in the key rod that in turn causes the key to break off when you try to straighten it. If this happens, unless you have an identical accordion from which to scavenge parts, your only remedy will be to make a new key by combining parts of the broken key and parts of another fairly similar key from some junk accordion. You simply cannot find an exact replacement key available for sale off the shelf.

Sometimes you will find a loose or missing bellows corner. If just one or two are loose, it may be an anomaly that can be easily fixed. However, if several are loose or missing, it is probably an indication that all the metal corners are fatigued and cracked and the rest will fall off soon. In this case the best solution is to get a new bellows.

These are the problems you are most likely to encounter. Nearly every old accordion will have one or more of these problems. Understanding how to identify these problems and how to estimate the cost to correct them is essential to determining the as-is value of any used accordion.

17.

Brand Names

We all want to rely on brand names as an indicator of quality, but in accordions, brand names don't mean much. There are hundreds of brand names, and the vast majority of them are just the name of the accordion teacher who imported them to sell to his students.

Sure, there are some well known brands, including Petosa, Giulietti, Scandalli, Sonola, Excelsior, Bell, Hohner, Pan, Titano, and others. However, keep in mind that these names are known and respected chiefly because of their top of the line professional models, while the vast majority of the accordions they made were of appropriate quality levels to satisfy demand from all the other segments of the market, including the largest segment of all, child beginners. Having a well known top of the line professional model does not mean that every accordion bearing that same brand name is of equal quality, because those other accordions were intentionally made to lower quality standards in order to meet lower price points appropriate to the market segments being targeted.

Even accordions bearing identical model names and numbers

can vary greatly in quality, because these models were made over a number of years, and included components from a variety of suppliers, some of whom changed their product or were replaced by other suppliers during the life of the model. Also relevant is the fact that all accordions are essentially custom-built by hand, with the quality dependent on the skill of the particular workers building that particular instrument.

No two accordions are alike. The major components of two supposedly identical accordions coming off the production line the same day are not necessarily interchangeable. For instance, the bass side of one accordion probably cannot simply be mounted to the treble side of a different accordion of the identical model coming off the production line the same day. This is because the accordion cabinet was originally made in one piece, and was later sawn in half to separate the treble side from the bass side.

Because no two cabinets are exactly the same, the two halves are numbered and kept together until the accordion is completed. As the assembly of the accordion progresses, many components are custom fitted by hand to each cabinet, including, reed blocks, bellows, treble keys, and bass buttons.

While each of these components can probably be modified to fit other accordions from the same assembly line, they are not directly interchangeable without some custom fitting. Even the reed blocks are custom fitted and often cannot simply be transferred to another supposedly identical accordion without making some modifications.

Every accordion is unique, and many of them were made to

a relatively low quality standard intended for beginners at entry level prices. Of course, there is great variation between them, so to judge the quality of any individual accordion, you must examine it closely, feel it, play it, and hear it. You cannot rely on any brand name alone as a guarantee of quality.

The only limited exception to this might be among the top of the line professional models, which were presumably made to more exacting standards to please knowledgeable professionals who demanded the best. However, no two of these are the same, either, so even though it is comforting to know you have an accordion that was built to higher standards, you still must see it, feel it, play it, and hear it to be sure it actually met (or still meets) those standards.

One important factor in support of these top of the line instruments, though, is that, unlike student models, they will almost always be worth repairing, because their potential market value will nearly always exceed the cost of repair, even of major repairs. Thus, even though significantly more costly, they may turn out to be among the best bargains if you ever try to get your money back by selling.

18.

Chinese Accordions

Although the vast majority of used accordions of all quality levels available in the United States are of Italian manufacture, today's Italian accordion manufacturers have largely retreated to the more upscale market segments, having conceded the lower market segments for new accordions to Chinese manufacturers.

I have read that there are more accordion players in China than in all other countries combined. To satisfy that huge market, as well as to export to the U.S. and other countries, China has become the world's largest accordion producer, and at low prices. A brand new full size 120/41 LMMH of Chinese manufacture can be purchased retail in the U.S. for about the same cost as a decent used Italian accordion of similar design.

Most people are suspicious of Chinese accordions, equating low price with inferior quality, but this is not necessarily a valid equation. Just as with brand names, the country of origin is not a reliable indicator of quality. While my experiences repairing Chinese accordions have been limited, I recently repaired a Chinese full size 120/41 LMMH that appears to be at least as well made as the typical Italian accordion, at a fraction of the cost.

Even though this accordion was only six or seven years old, many of the leathers were already curled and needed replacing. This could be an indication that inferior quality leather was used, but it could also be due to the conditions under which the accordion has been played and stored. Moisture, heat, temperature changes, and condensation are the enemies of leather, and could account for the premature failure.

But even assuming that inferior materials caused the problem, I still think the owner of this accordion got a bargain. He had paid less than $1,000 for it brand new. It has a good sound and he has played it for six or seven years with no problems, until finally a bass button stuck down and one of his treble reed leathers got bad enough to throw its reed out of tune. For a couple hundred bucks, I repaired his bass machine (which was removable as a unit, making access quick and easy) and changed all the bad leathers, and now he is back in business. I would not be ashamed to own that accordion. It appears to be of equivalent quality to the Italian accordions that most of us play.

I have also seen one Chinese accordion that was built so cheaply that I would not want to own it. However, this was a smaller model that was purchased new for just a couple hundred dollars, so I assume it was intentionally built as cheaply as possible to satisfy that market segment.

I'm betting that the Chinese will eventually do with accordions what the Japanese did with electronics and automobiles. Japanese manufacturers originally produced bottom of the line goods that we all thought of as junk, but once they got their foothold in foreign markets, they continually improved until today many Japanese products are widely recognized as the world's best. Don't be surprised if someday soon, the best accordions come from China. And don't be afraid to buy a Chinese accordion now, as long as you inspect it carefully, or have it inspected by a knowledgeable accordion repair person to make an informed assessment of its quality and condition, just as you would do with any other accordion.

19.

Sound Quality

The sound of an accordion is the single most important factor to consider when buying. To a large extent, the evaluation must be subjective, based on your personal taste, but there are some objective comparisons that can be made.

One objective parameter is dynamic range. How softly will it play, and how loudly will it play without the notes going flat? These limits define the accordion's dynamic range. Accordions with higher quality reeds generally have a broader dynamic range, but reed block design and accordion cabinet design are also important.

Sound quality depends on many factors, including reed quality, reed wax condition, reed block design and anchorage, types of wood used, and cabinet design and construction. The accordion cabinet is like the sound board of a piano. Even the best reeds emit a pathetically weak sound until they are anchored to this resonant structure. The vibrating reed transmits its vibrations to the accordion cabinet through the wax, the reed block, and the foundation plate. The volume and quality of the sound we hear depend to a large extent on how effectively these vibrations are transmitted, and the sound we hear emanates as much from the accordion cabinet as from the reed. You can feel the accordion cabinet vibrate against your chest as you play. I know of no way to visually determine how well these vibrations will be transmitted, or to predict what quality of sound will result. The only way to find out is by listening.

Accordions either with tone chambers or with musette tuning are usually capable of louder sound. In the case of tone chambers, this is probably due to the tone chamber itself vibrating in reaction to the reed vibrations transmitted to and through it. In the case of musette tuning, it is the result of the two slightly differently tuned reeds coming into phase several times each second, thereby increasing the volume several times per second to create the tremolo effect (for a more thorough explanation of this, see Chapter 27).

Especially if you intend to play unamplified outdoors or in large rooms, loud volume is important. On the other hand, if you play in your apartment with close neighbors late at night, it may be important to be able to play very softly. Accordions with the best dynamic range offer the best flexibility for playing in different environments.

As for subjectively evaluating the sound, you might notice whether it is clear and brassy, or mellow and muted. Some accordions sound a bit nasal, some deep and resonant. These are all matters of personal taste, but some accordions sound harsh to just about everyone's ear, which is usually an indication that reeds are out of tune.

Be aware that accordions can sound differently to people out in front of them than they do to the player. I learned this lesson a few years ago when I sold for a pittance an accordion whose sound I did not care for. The buyer loved the sound of it and snapped it up at the low price I offered him. But then when I heard him play it, I liked the sound, too. It clearly sounded very differently from out in front.

I experienced the opposite side of this in the Beltuna factory showroom in Castelfidardo. The factory showroom demonstrator I played sounded magnificent, even better than either my Giulietti Classic 127 or my Giulietti Super, both of which I love. I thought I simply must buy this accordion because it sounds so good when I play it.

However, having learned my lesson earlier, I had another accordion player play it for me while I listened from out in front. From out there, it sounded just like my Giulietti accordions. Apparently, Beltuna has figured out a way to deliver the best sound to the player, rather than to the audience. The grille openings on the back of the accordion may provide a clue to how they accomplished that. At any rate, since I was no longer convinced that the overall Beltuna sound quality was superior to Giulietti's, I was able to resist the purchase, at least so far.

The bottom line is that you should listen to your prospective new accordion from out in front of it as well as from behind.

20.

What Should I Buy?

This is the main question, isn't it? Naturally, the answer will depend on why you are buying it, and what you are going to do with it.

If you are a beginner buying your first accordion in order to learn to play on it, my advice is not to spend too much money, because your taste in accordions is probably going to change anyway, as you gain more experience and familiarity. In this case, try to buy one that sounds good to you and that is in reasonably good condition, so you won't have to spend a lot on repairing it (or pay a low price so you can afford to fix it and still stay within budget), but don't spring for a top of the line model with handmade reeds. If you are a beginner, it will probably be a while before you can hear and feel the differences, anyway, so why pay extra for them? If you are a student, buy a student accordion.

If you stick with it, you will eventually just naturally acquire more accordions, so you can always get a better one later. The money you spend on the starter accordion will not be lost, because you will continue to use it as a backup, or as a travel accordion, or as one you can play at the beach without fretting too much about the damage the salt air might do to the reeds. Every accordion player eventually needs more than one accordion.

If you have been playing for a while and are thinking of upgrading, or buying a backup accordion, think about diversifying. If you already have a dry tuned accordion, why not get a musette accordion? If you already have a heavy accordion, why not get a light one for strolling? If you don't already have an antique accordion, why not get one and rebuild it or have it rebuilt? If you are no longer happy with the reed response of your old one, look for one with better reeds.

If you like to play standing up, then don't buy one that is too heavy. If you like to play in large rooms or outdoors, get one that can play loudly. If you love French or Italian musette waltzes, *ballo liscio*, or other folk music, be sure to get one that is musette tuned.

If you are dead set on buying a professional quality instrument, and you are sure you know which one is right for you, then do it. If it is in good condition and you care for it properly, you will probably be able to get your money back out of it when and if you ever decide to sell it. But meanwhile, you will have a lot of money tied up. And, as you gain experience, your tastes may change, making some other professional model more attractive.

If you are buying an accordion with the intention of repairing it and reselling it for a profit, then I advise buying better quality, because the cost of repairing it is less likely to exceed its eventual resale value.

If you are already so familiar with accordions that you know what you want, and you are buying a keeper because you love the looks, sound, and feel of it, then you probably are not reading this guide. But in case you are, I will offer just one bit of advice. Don't worry much about the cost. If it will bring you happiness, happiness is priceless, so get exactly what you want and fix it up exactly the way you like it. You only live once.

21.

Where Should I Look?

Everyone looks on eBay, and you can find some interesting accordions there, but the big drawback is that you can't play the accordion before you buy it. No matter how good it looks in the photos, you are taking a big chance. Most eBay sellers allow no returns, and most know nothing about the accordions they are selling. In most cases, they are selling junk, and if you buy their junk, you're stuck with it. If you buy on eBay, assume the worst, and you won't be far off. Assume everything is wrong with the accordion that they don't specifically say is not wrong, and pay accordingly. If you do that, you won't be too disappointed when it arrives.

Of course, there are also some knowledgeable sellers on eBay, and you can tell who they are by looking at the photos they provide and by reading what they say in their listing. You want to see very clear, high resolution photos of all reed blocks, because this is a sign that the seller knows how an accordion works, what generally goes wrong, and what knowledgeable buyers will need to know before buying. You also want the seller to have written that the accordion has been professionally refurbished and is in perfect condition, and that you can return it if you are not pleased with it.

Barring that, at the very least you want the seller to say every leather is soft and flat against the reed plate, every note in every register is sweet and clear, that it is in perfect tune, etc. If the seller is willing to make specific representations backed by his/her eBay reputation, then you are probably safe to believe them and bid accordingly. After all, if the seller misrepresents the accordion, you will give negative feedback, and no eBay dealer wants that. The point is, do not assume the best, and do not pay for anything the seller will not clearly confirm, backed by his/her eBay reputation.

Other sources are the accordion dealers with relatively large inventories and informative websites like Castiglione, Accordions International, Defner, Petosa, Accordion Lab, etc. Naturally, you want the same assurances, guarantees, and return privileges if you are going to pay anything close to their asking prices.

The Cotati Accordion Festival and other similar festivals and conventions around the country are good places to look. Here, you can actually see the accordion and play it. You can have the seller open it up for you (i.e., split it at the bellows to expose the reed blocks) so you can see for yourself if any leathers are curled, or if the wax is brittle, or if any reeds are rusted.

Local accordion clubs are full of members who have accordions to sell. Just go to a meeting, or call the club president and mention you are looking for an accordion, and you will be besieged with opportunities. However, be aware that most accordion players don't know much more about their accordions than you do.

Before buying one of these, you should have it checked out by a competent accordion repair person who will provide an estimate of repair costs.

Music stores often have used accordions for sale, but some may not be knowledgeable enough about accordions to ensure that what they are selling you is actually in good condition. If they sell a lot of accordions and have an accordion repair person on staff, your chances are pretty good, but if they just sell one once in a while and rely on outside repair services, you should be extra cautious.

I was in a music store once when the itinerant accordion repairman arrived to repair one of the store's accordions, and I witnessed him make some down and dirty quick fix repairs. He was clearly knowledgeable, skillful, and fast, but was apparently doing only the absolute minimum to get the thing working, which is probably just what the music store had requested. That's not the kind of accordion you want to buy for a high price.

Consignment stores sometimes accept accordions, but the shop owners usually know nothing about them and cannot make any guarantees, so you are on your own. Antique stores often have them, too, but I have never seen anything there but junk. They seem to think people will buy old accordion hulks just as ornaments, and in most cases, that is their only value.

Remember the main thrust of Chapter 1 was that total cost equals purchase price plus cost of repairs, and all old accordions need repairs. Regardless of where you look for an accordion, never pay "good condition" prices for accordions that are not in good condition, and never buy any accordion without looking inside, or having your repair person look inside, or at the very least, having a knowledgeable seller look inside and make specific representations and warranties about what he/she saw there (unless you are assuming you will be getting junk and are paying junk prices).

22.

How Can I Determine its Condition?

When you are checking out an accordion to buy, do as I do when I perform a condition inspection report for customers. You can use the inspection form printed in the back of this guide as a checklist. I begin by describing the accordion, including listing the manufacturer, model, cabinet color, bellows color, accordion size category, number of treble and bass keys, keyboard length, reed configuration, and weight.

I perform an exterior visual inspection and note its general appearance, bellows condition (leaks, missing corners, worn bellows tape, stains, etc.) keyboard condition (cracks, scratches, stains, out of level, wobbly keys, etc.), grille condition (dents, cracks, looseness, missing parts, rust), switch functions, shoulder strap condition, and bass strap condition. I sniff it and note any lingering odors of mildew, cigarette smoke, perfume, etc.

I use the treble switches to isolate and play every reed individually in both bellows directions and make note of any sticking keys, silent reeds, bad leathers, serious tuning problems, etc. I listen for and note any unnaturally loud keyboard mechanical noises.

I play the accordion and note whether it is wet or dry tuned and I comment on the general sound quality. As I play I check the bellows for air tightness, and note any problems. I check the reed response and rate it as poor, normal, or excellent. I note whether the reeds are properly voiced, i.e., if some seem slow to respond, or if they choke on high bellows pressure. If it has internal microphones and a standard RCA jack, I check the microphones for proper operation. (Naturally, this requires plugging into an amplifier.)

I notice and report my subjective impressions of keyboard length, key width, and key travel (do my fingers fit between the black keys? Does the keyboard fit my hand? Do I like the depth of action?). I listen and feel for any air leaks and note their likely location and cause.

I remove the treble grille and check the condition of the grille anchorage, grille cloth, treble valves, key rods, and switch mechanisms, and note whether treble keys are individually removable (individually removable keys make for easier maintenance).

I remove the bellows pins and split the accordion to check the condition of the reeds (rusty? dusty? grimy? handmade?), reed wax (brittle or cracked?), and leathers (curled? dry and hard?). I remove the reed blocks and use a headlamp to visually check the condition of the interior leathers, noting approximately how many should be replaced. I note whether the switch slides are mounted in the reed blocks or in the foundation plates, whether all reed blocks are tightly mounted, whether the interior is clean or dirty, and the interior condition of the bellows (punctures, wear, cracked glue, broken microphone wires, etc.).

I remove the bass cover and visually inspect the bass machine, noting the condition of the buttons and pistons, whether all the pins on the pistons are engaged with their levers, whether there is excessive slack in the button linkages, whether any of the wood mounting is cracked or loose, whether there is dirt or corrosion that might affect the operation, whether the bass buttons and valves are inordinately noisy, and whether the bass machine is removable as a unit (which allows easier maintenance).

I check the bass strap bottom anchor and top adjustment screw for security and proper operation. I check the condition of the bass grille cloth and note whether there are any internal microphones on the bass side.

I determine the type of case (hard or soft) and its condition, noting any problems with hinges, latches, handles, interior liners, and exterior appearance.

Finally, I write a condition report detailing all of the above items, and include a cost estimate for any recommended repairs, separating repairs into essential and elective categories. The whole process takes about two hours, but by the end I have a good feel for the quality and condition of the accordion, its approximate value as is, and its potential value after repairs are made.

If you make a similar inspection and compare what you find to what you find in other accordions, you will have a good idea of their relative values. You might want to use the accordion condition inspection report in the back of this book as a guide.

23.

How Picky Should I Be?

In terms of general sound quality, you should be very picky. A sour note or two can probably be easily remedied, but if you don't like the overall sound of the accordion, there is not much to be done about that, so don't buy it at any price.

In terms of reed configuration, be very picky. Hold out for what you want. There are plenty of accordions of all reed configurations constantly coming on the market, so there is no reason to settle for second best.

Similarly, not much can be done to improve weight and balance, so be sure to buy only what you want. Keep in mind the compromises that must be made in order to build a light weight accordion, and buy the compromise that is best for you.

In terms of keyboard feel, you can be more flexible. Keyboard action can be improved. Just keep in mind the cost of this when deciding how much to pay.

You can also be a bit flexible with cosmetic issues. Minor scratches and fogging of the celluloid finish can sometimes be buffed out. Bass buttons and treble keys can be shined up on a buffing wheel. However, yellowed treble keys can usually not be whitened without replacing the plastic key tops, which is a time-consuming operation, so take the cost of this into consideration when you buy. A previous owner's name on the front of the accordion usually cannot be completely removed, because most were set with glue that attacks the celluloid finish, leaving a faint impression of the letters in the accordion finish even after the letters are removed.

In terms of general condition, how picky you should be depends on what price you are paying. It's okay to buy an accordion needing repairs (nearly all do!), as long as you understand the extent and likely cost of those repairs. Does it need new reed leathers, new reed wax, a new bellows, new shoulder straps and bass strap, etc? Just have a repair person prepare a cost estimate for the repairs and factor that into the price you pay.

Sometimes it may even be better to buy one needing repairs, for several reasons:

1) The fact that the current owner has not personally valued the accordion highly enough to pay for those repairs himself suggests that he just does not want it anymore, and might be willing to sell it at a bargain price.

2) If the price has been reduced by enough to pay for these repairs and you go ahead with them, then you will have a freshly repaired

accordion which is far better than one that had no price reduction simply because those repairs were not quite needed yet.

3) Sometimes during those repairs modifications can be made at little or no additional cost to customize the accordion more to your liking. For instance, if it needs a new bellows, you get to pick the color. If necessary repairs already include dismantling the keyboard and leveling it upon reassembly, you can probably have it set to a shallower action at no extra cost. As long as you keep in mind that total cost includes the cost of repairs and pay accordingly, you will end up with good value.

24.

How Much Should I Pay?

Quoting specific prices in a book that may be around for many years is dicey, at best, because we live in inflationary times. Any price I quote today might be obsolete tomorrow, so I'm going to qualify all the prices I mention as follows.

First, this was written in California in May 2012, when the latest San Francisco consumer price index for all urban consumers (CPI-U) for April 2012 was 230.085. To get a rough idea of what the price might be by the time you read this, you might inflate any price I mention by applying the percentage shift in the CPI since April 2012. However, that may not be sufficient, because other factors may have shifted the cost of used accordions and/or the cost of the materials and skills used in accordion repair, upwards or downwards relative to the CPI. These factors include general demand for accordions, relative scarcity of specific types, and currency exchange rates (most accordion parts and new accordions come from Italy). My point is that the only accordion purchase and repair prices that will have any enduring meaning are relative prices within the accordion world.

As I write this, for top of the line professional quality accordions, Petosa in Seattle is offering a brand new Giulietti Classic 127 (41/120 LMMH with tone chamber and handmade reeds) for $9900. Castiglione in Warren, Michigan, is offering a similar accordion, the Beltuna Leader IV (41/120 LMMH with tone chamber and handmade reeds) for $9500.

For accordions one step down the ladder, at least in reed quality, Accordions International is offering a LMMH or LMMM (your choice) Piermaria 212 full size accordion with hand finished reeds for $8400.

For smaller accordions, Accordions USA in Clifton, New Jersey is offering a Moreschi 37/96 4/5 LMMH with tone chamber and handmade reeds for $6995, and Accordions International in Salt Lake City is offering a Piermaria 210 LMMH or LMMM 37/96 (no tone chamber, export quality machine made reeds) at a list price of $7025.

A complete set of Binci handmade reeds for a 120/41 LMM 3/5 accordion can be imported for just under $1300, including freight and customs charges.

All the above are Italian accordions and reeds, and the prices offered in dollars are naturally dependent on the dollar/euro exchange rate, which is currently at US$1.30. Any prices listed below should be adjusted to reflect any changes in the pricing environment just described.

In today's price environment, I'm suggesting that to get a normal used accordion in reasonably good condition you should probably expect to pay a total cost (purchase price plus needed repairs) in the following ranges shown for the various reed configurations.

12-bass 2-reed	LM or MM	$200 to $300
120/41 2-reed	LM or MM	$400 to $800
120/41 3-reed	LMH	$600 to $1,000
120/41 3-reed	LMM musette	$800 to $2000
120/41 4-reed	LMMM musette	$1,200 to $3,000
120/41 4-reed	LMMH	$1,200 to $3,000

For a professional quality instrument in reasonably good condition with tone chamber and handmade reeds, you should expect to pay $4,000 to $6,000. Although I have seen listings in the $3,000 range, they are rare, and probably reflect the need for repairs.

Naturally, you should expect to pay significantly more than the prices listed above for instruments in excellent condition. In today's pricing environment (2012), a used professional quality full size 120/41 LMMH accordion with tone chamber and handmade reeds in excellent condition is probably going to cost between $6,000 and $8,000

I define "reasonably good condition" as fully functional and playable, sounding reasonably good, and having no major cosmetic flaws. That means having all reeds sounding properly, no reeds glaringly out of tune, no noisy leathers, no major air leaks, no treble key more than 1/32 inch higher than the others, no broken keys or buttons, no cracked key tops, no sticking keys or buttons, intact bellows tape and bellows corners, no major scratches or cracks in the celluloid finish, and no inoperable treble or bass switches.

Note that "reasonably good condition" addresses only how the accordion is today, and says nothing about its likely durability or repairs that may be needed in the future. An accordion with brittle reed wax, marginal leathers, stiff and hardened felt pads under keys and on valve pallets, minor internal and external air leaks, old brittle bellows corners, discolored bellows fabric, yellowed keys, little spots of rust on the chrome trim, and minor scratches might very well fit this definition of "reasonably good condition" and still require major expensive repairs to put it in "excellent condition". However, it probably does not need to be in excellent condition for you to get a lot of use and enjoyment out of it.

I define "excellent condition" as like new. An accordion in excellent condition has a nearly flawless appearance, very tight bellows with no discernible air leaks, flawless bellows tape and bellows corners, smooth, quiet, perfectly level keyboard, quiet bass machine, and flawless tuning and voicing. A used accordion in truly excellent condition can be worth nearly as much as a similar new one.

The problem is getting the old one into truly excellent condition. This often means new wax and leathers, new bass and treble valves, re-leveling the keyboard, installing new bellows, and extensive tuning. Sometimes the keyboard needs to be overhauled and/or have new key tops installed. The cost of all these repairs can bring your total cost up close to the cost of buying a similar new accordion.

Finally, don't forget about shoulder straps, bass strap, bellows straps, and the accordion case. Most old accordions come with old shoulder straps, too narrow for comfort, and sometimes dangerously rotten and weak. They often come with ratty, broken cases or no case at all. If your prospective purchase has new straps and a good solid case, you can afford to pay more for it. New cases run $100 to $150, new wide shoulder straps cost $75 to $125, and a new bass strap runs around $40 installed.

To summarize, you should expect to pay more for more sets of reeds, more for musette tuning, more for a tone chamber, more for handmade reeds, more for accordions in excellent condition, and a little more for good straps and case. If the condition of your accordion lies somewhere between "reasonably good condition" and "excellent condition" it should be priced accordingly.

25.

Calculating the Number of Reeds

How many reeds does your accordion contain? This is an important question because the costs of certain kinds of repairs are roughly proportional to the number of reeds. Each of the treble reed sets contains one reed for each treble key on the accordion. In other words, in the case of 41-key accordions, 2-reed accordions have 82 reeds on the treble side, 3-reed accordions have 123, 4-reed accordions have 164, and 5-reed accordions have 205. In addition, each of the bass reed sets contains 12 reeds, so a typical 4/5 accordion (5 bass reed sets) has 164 reeds on the treble side and 60 on the bass side and for a total of 224, while a 2/4 accordion has just 130.

The greater complexity of the larger accordions contributes not only to their initial price, but also to the cost of repairs. For example, on all but a few notes at the high end of the keyboard, each reed tongue (two reed tongues per reed) has a leather reed valve mounted over its slot in the reed plate. Replacing these leathers is the most commonly needed repair. On a 41/120 LMMH accordion, there are around 420 leathers to change, which is a time-consuming job. Even more time is required to change all the leathers on a 5/5 accordion, while far less time is required on a 2/4 accordion.

Extended keyboard accordions have more than 41 reeds in each treble set, and thus a greater total number of reeds. The point is that using the examples above, you can calculate the number of reeds in your accordion and thereby estimate how expensive or inexpensive it will be to change the leathers, re-wax the reeds, or tune the reeds, relative to other accordions.

26.

Identifying Handmade Reeds

To shed some light on the differences between handmade reeds and other grades, I visited Binci in Castelfidardo, Italy. I was wondering why Binci's handmade reeds are widely reputed to be better than machine made reeds. After all, shouldn't today's computer controlled machinery be able to make reeds more consistently and to closer tolerances than any mortal human using only hand and eye?

Claudio Binci very graciously gave me a tour of his shop and let me watch him make a reed, which he then gave me as a souvenir. To find out why Binci handmade reeds might be better than standard reeds, I compared the reed Binci made for me with a machine made reed of the same frequency taken from a junk accordion (the lowest treble E, denoted as #7 on the Italian accordion makers chart). I used a 15x binocular microscope, a dial caliper, and feeler gauges to identify the differences.

Binci handmade reed (left) and machine made reed

In general appearance, they are very similar, except the edges of the Binci reed plate are smoother and more cleanly cut. Binci's reed vent and tapered reed tongue are only about 4% shorter in length, and about 10% wider near the base. The tip width of Binci's reed tongue is a mere .002" narrower than the standard reed tongue, while the square fixed ends of both reeds are identical in both width and thickness.

As you can see in the photos below, the fixed end of Binci's reed tongue has blue edges, an indication that the reed blank was stamped from a coil of blued spring steel just one reed wide, while the edges at the base of the standard reed are a bare shiny steel color, because it was stamped from a coil eight reeds wide. Mr. Binci took me to a nearby factory where the reed plates and reed blanks are made, and showed me the stamping machinery and both coils. According to him, the single reed-width coil is spring steel of a higher quality than the wider coil. It is blue on all sides until cut or filed by the stamping machine or the reed maker. Two identical reed blanks are stamped out as Siamese twins, joined end to end at the base, and the reed maker later cuts them apart and uses one on each side of the reed plate. Because this bottom edge where they are cut apart is not an outer edge of the coil, it is not blue, even on the Binci handmade reed. The edges along both sides of the base, though, are blue, as you can see.

Binci handmade reed base with uncut blue edge.

Machine made reed base with cut edge

Binci's reed plate is made from a harder aluminum alloy called duraluminum which, as he demonstrated, can easily scratch the softer aluminum reed plate of the standard reed, while the standard aluminum reed plate cannot be made to scratch the harder duraluminum Binci reed plate. The common wisdom is that the harder reed plate allows a tighter and more durable rivet connection of the reed tongue to the reed plate. This enhances frequency stability by discouraging the reed tongue from lifting and bringing more of the reed tongue's length into oscillation during loud playing (a longer vibrating element vibrates at a slower rate). Some experts feel the harder duraluminum more efficiently transmits reed vibration to the reed block, producing a louder, fuller sound. In addition, the duraluminum survives the stamping process without spalling in the vent slots whereas the softer aluminum reed plate exhibits spalling in those areas.

Other differences appear in the filing. The un-filed full thickness blue tip of Binci's reed is 60% longer than that of the standard reed. The standard reed tongue has a smoother finish, while Binci's reed looks slightly rougher. Rocking both reeds under a bright light reveals the standard reed tongue to be very flat, reflecting with consistent brightness across its width, while the bright spots on Binci's reed tongue dance around a bit, revealing a slightly wavy or faceted surface. Examination under a 15X microscope also reveals distinct and uneven file marks on Binci's reed, while the standard reed exhibits a more uniformly ground surface.

As you can see in the photos below, the taper from the deeply filed area up to the undisturbed blue surface at the tip of Binci's reed is much more abrupt, ramping up .010 inch over a horizontal distance of about .030 inch while the taper on the standard reed is 9 or 10 times that long, difficult to measure because it is so gradual, and more of a continuous curve than an abrupt ramp.

Close-up of Binci hand filed reed tip

Close-up of machine ground reed tip.

The side clearance between Binci's reed tongue and the reed vent (the slot in the reed plate, through which the reed tongue vibrates) is just half that on the standard reed (.0015" versus .0030"). The deeply filed portion of Binci's reed is 31% thinner (.011" versus .016" for the machine made reed). Under 15X magnification, the interior surfaces of Binci's reed vent look pretty smooth, while on the standard reed plate they appear rough and pitted due to spalling during the stamping process.

It is no wonder that Binci's reed requires less air to get it moving. The longer un-filed tip puts the center of gravity farther out, allowing the lower part of the reed tongue to be thinner, and the entire reed to be lighter, yet still vibrate at the correct frequency. A thinner and lighter reed tongue has less inertia and therefore requires less energy to get it moving. Tighter and more uniform clearance around the reed tongue in the reed vent reduces air leakage around the reed, putting more of the moving air's energy to work driving the reed. These two factors: 1) less energy required to activate the lighter reed, and 2) more energy extracted from every bit of moving air, compound synergistically to require much less air to activate the Binci handmade reed.

So what is Binci's secret? I don't believe it lies in the hand-making as much as it lies in reed design, primarily in the lower mass of the reed tongue, the closer fit, and probably also in selection of higher grade materials. For instance, a higher grade of steel may be required to make this thinner reed tongue sufficiently durable. The duraluminum reed plate may make it easier to produce smoother, more uniform reed vents, and may be more stable under the stress of riveting the reed tongue in place. I think using this same design and these same materials, computer controlled machinery could probably do an equally good job of making consistently high quality reeds.

Not all handmade reeds exhibit all the features found in the Binci reed, and I suspect this may be due to some considerable latitude being taken regarding the use of the term "handmade" as an indication of the highest grade or quality, rather than as a warranty that it was actually filed by hand. For instance, many handmade reeds appear just as smoothly ground as the machine made reed above, and many also have the machine made reed's gradual taper up to the unfiled tip. Some also have the file/grinding marks made diagonally across the width of the reed tongue, rather than straight across. Are these indications that the reed was actually machine ground? I feel pretty sure they are.

However, many of the Binci reeds are also initially machine ground to the approximate required thickness as well, and then hand filed to final dimensions. Mr. Binci gave me one of these "Siamese twin" reed blanks for one of the higher notes that he took from a supply bin in his workshop. It was already ground to the approximate final shape before the master reed maker ever touched it, and under magnification it reveals the same fine textured, perfectly uniform grinding marks of the machine made reed.

Regardless of the variations in technique or in the latitude taken in applying the term "handmade" by various reed makers, the universal identifying characteristics of handmade reeds are the blue uncut edges at the sides of the bases of all handmade reed tongues and the harder duraluminum reed plates used in making handmade reeds. The other differences, such as faceting and rougher file marks, contribute nothing to quality, but merely offer visual clues as to how the reeds were made. What really counts is how thin and light the reed tongue is, and how well it fits the reed vent.

The bottom line is that good reeds enhance an accordion's value. Some accordions have better reeds than others. Finding hand-made reeds in an accordion is a good indication that they ought to perform well, but you can only determine that by playing the accordion and comparing the reed response to that of other accordions.

You can identify handmade reeds visually by confirming they have these features:

- Blue edges at the base, sometimes hard to see in poor light, prove the reed blank was stamped from the one-reed-wide coil. This is a universal feature of handmade reeds and is an indication of the best quality steel.

- Slightly faceted tongues that show up when you rotate the reed under bright light are evidence of hand filing, but are not necessarily an indication of higher quality.

- Rougher and less uniform file marks that show up under magnification are more evidence of hand filing, but also not necessarily an indication of higher quality.

- Tighter clearances between the reed tongue and the reed vent are an indication of high quality, but hand fitted reeds (the next grade down) also have this tighter clearance.

- Thinner cross section of the reed tongue along most of its length is a universal characteristic of handmade reeds, but varies in degree from one reed maker to another.

- Abrupt transitions from thin filed sections to the unfiled tip of the reed tongue are more evidence of hand filing, but this difference exists only on the larger reeds, as the smaller ones have no unfiled tip. Not all handmade reeds exhibit this abrupt transition, even on the reeds where unfiled tips exist.

- Smoother surfaces inside the reed vents are a universal characteristic of the duraluminum reed plates used for handmade reeds.

- You can test the hardness of the reed plate by trying to scratch one reed plate with another. Aluminum reed plates will very lightly scratch other aluminum reed plates, but will not scratch duraluminum at all. Duraluminum reed plates will only very lightly scratch other duraluminum plates, but will easily and quite clearly and deeply scratch standard aluminum reed plates. As far as I know, duraluminum has so far been used only on handmade reeds, but that does not mean this will always be the case. There is nothing to prevent someone from mating a machine made reed tongue to a duraluminum reed plate.

Binci reed

Now you can visually identify handmade reeds with certainty, but don't let visual identification be your only guide. You should also demand that the reeds actually perform noticeably better before you pay extra for them.

27.

Intricacies of Musette Tuning

If you are looking for a Musette tuned accordion, then you should understand the available options, and the differences between various musette accordions, as there are many. Naturally, you will want to know whether the musette accordion you are considering has two sets of M reeds or three. However, there is great variety in musette tuning, even among accordions with only two M sets. In fact, many accordions with two M sets are dry tuned, with no tremolo at all. Those that are wet tuned vary not only in their degree of wetness, but also in their beat progression. I will explain these terms (wetness and beat progression) one at a time, but first, let's understand "tremolo".

Accordions with no tremolo are said to be dry, while those with tremolo are said to be wet. You can hear the tremolo as a "wah-wah-wah-wah" sound, with each "wah" being a pulse or beat of louder volume, usually from one to ten beats per second. Accordions (or notes) with a faster tremolo beat are said to be wetter, those with a slower tremolo beat are said to be dryer.

The tremolo we hear is actually a series of variations in volume due to two different sound frequencies coming periodically into phase with each other. Think of a sound wave as a rapidly alternating series of high and low air pressures reaching your ear. When two such waves are in phase with each other, that is, when the high pressure points in both their waves reach your ear simultaneously, they augment one another, causing you to hear a louder sound. If they are 180 degrees out of phase, that is, if the high point of one reaches your ear at the same time as the low point of the other, they tend to cancel each other out, and you hear a weaker sound. When two waves are of very nearly the same frequency, but not exactly the same, they periodically come into and out of phase with each other, causing you to hear first the louder sound, then the weaker sound, then the louder, etc., in rapid succession, as they go in and out of phase. We call this rapid variation in volume "tremolo", or sometimes "vibrato".

If two sounds vary by one vibration per second (i.e., one hertz), they come into phase once per second, causing you to hear a tremolo beat of 1 beat per second. If they vary by exactly two hertz, then they come into phase twice per second, causing you to hear a tremolo of two beats per second. If they are 10 hertz apart in frequency, you hear a tremolo beat of 10 bps, and so on. You can see the truth of this by considering a specific example.

Consider one note at 100 hertz and another at 102 hertz. If both tones begin at the same instant, then they are exactly in phase on the first oscillation, that is, during the first 1/100 of a second you hear the loudest sound. As they continue to vibrate at their respective frequencies, they gradually get more and more out of phase (because one is vibrating slightly faster), and the sound grows steadily weaker until after exactly ¼ second, they are completely out of phase and the sound is weakest because one has completed exactly 25 vibration cycles, while the other has completed 25.5 vibration cycles, putting them ½ cycle apart.

Under this condition the low pressure point of one wave arrives at the ear simultaneously with the high pressure point of the other. At this point in the cycle they tend to cancel each other out and we hear the weakest volume. However, immediately after this point they begin to come back into phase until at the half-second point they are precisely back into phase because one has completed exactly 50 vibration cycles and the other has completed exactly 51, once again causing the pressure peaks of each wave to arrive at the ear at the same instant, producing the loudest sound.

This cycle is repeated during the second half second and during each half second thereafter, causing us to hear a tremolo beat of 2 bps. If the two tones are 3 hertz apart, this cycle repeats each 1/3 second, producing a tremolo beat of 3 bps. If they are 10 hertz apart, the cycle repeats each 1/10 second, producing a tremolo beat of 10 bps. The general case is that for any two tones n hertz apart, a tremolo beat of n bps will be generated. (By the way, this generalization holds true for large differences, too. For instance, if two tones are 110 hertz apart, the "beat" will be at 110 bps, i.e., 110 hertz, which is in the audible range and is heard as an overtone A.)

"Wet" and "wetness" describe the intensity of the tremolo rather imprecisely. We can more precisely define the tremolo in terms of bps (beats per second), which leads us to the meaning of "beat progression".

Accordions most pleasing to the ear have slower tremolo beat frequencies on the lower notes, gradually increasing to faster beat frequencies on the higher notes. The rate at which the beat frequency increases as we move up the scale is what I call the beat progression. For instance, on my favorite accordion the beat progresses smoothly from 1 bps at the lowest F to 6 bps at the highest A, with a gradual increase of about 1/8 bps for each half step up the chromatic scale. Of course, our ears cannot detect such small differences as 1/8 bps, but as long as the tremolo beat frequency is perceived to increase gradually and evenly, while not reaching too high a frequency at the high end, the accordion will sound good.

Significant deviations from this smooth progression stand out as notes that "sing" out of tune because they beat at too high or too low a frequency relative to their neighbors. Any note that has a noticeably different tremolo beat from that of its immediate neighbors will sound out of tune as you play the scale, and this is one of the things you should watch out for on a musette accordion, as tuning is time consuming and expensive. Ideally, you want an accordion in which the tremolo beat increases steadily as you advance up the chromatic scale, and one in which the beats at the highest notes are not too fast for your personal taste and for the kind of music you will be playing.

The degree of wetness, i.e., the tremolo beat frequency, is determined by the degree of difference in tuning between the two sets of reeds. Because tuning equipment measures this degree of difference in tuning in terms of cents, musette tuning is often described in terms of cents.

A cent is 1/100 of a semitone, a semitone being the interval between any two adjacent notes in the chromatic scale. Thus, any two adjacent notes on the chromatic scale are 100 cents apart. You will often see references to musette tuning of 10 cents, or 15 cents, or even 20 cents or 25 cents. This supposedly means that one of the M sets of reeds is tuned 10 cents (or 15, 20, or 25 cents) sharper or flatter than the other set.

However, describing wetness in terms of a certain number of cents is an oversimplification because we are unlikely to find an accordion with all the pairs of notes in both sets of M reeds tuned to the same number of cents apart. When we do, they usually sound terrible on the higher notes because the tremolo beat is too fast, and if the cents of difference is set low enough so the beat is not too fast on the higher notes, then it seems too slow on the lower notes.

To avoid this problem, the higher notes must be tuned to fewer cents apart than the lower notes. This occurs because at the higher notes each cent has a greater impact on the tremolo beat frequency (see "Drilling down", below, for an explanation of why this is true). For instance, my favorite accordion is tuned to 5 cents sharp at the lowest F and 3 cents sharp at the highest A. It is not very informative to say it is tuned 5 cents wet because that is true only at the lowest note.

To avoid this oversimplification we could describe musette tuning in terms of the number of cents difference at both ends of the keyboard, but I think it is more informative to describe it in terms of the tremolo beat frequency, since that is what we actually hear. For instance, I generally say my favorite accordion's beat progresses from 1 bps at the low end to 6 bps at the high end, which describes it perfectly. If you tell me your accordion progresses linearly from 2 bps at the low end to 10 bps at the high end, I will know exactly what it sounds like, and that it is considerably wetter than mine. If you tell me that yours progresses from 2 bps at the low end to 6 bps in the middle, than stays level at 6 bps from there on up, I will understand exactly what you mean. If you say it has 12 bps at the high end, I will know that I will not like it, because it is too wet for my taste. It is far more informative to describe musette tuning in terms of the beat progression.

The fact that there are so many different tuning possibilities helps explain why no two accordions sound exactly alike. Personal taste varies greatly, and different beat progressions appeal to different people and different cultures. If you like the sound of one accordion better than another, it is probably at least partly because of the differences in their beat progressions. Identifying, understanding, and properly describing the beat progression will help you find the accordion that is right for you.

Most of the discussion until now has been about accordions with two sets of M reeds, because they are the most common. However, accordions with three M sets are called "full musette" accordions. In most of these models, one M set is tuned to concert pitch, one M set is tuned slightly sharp, and one M set is tuned slightly flat. However, in some cases both the second and third M sets are tuned sharp, with one being tuned slightly more sharp than the other. These models (MMM, LMMM, and LMMMH accordions) usually have a switch that allows playing just two of the M sets for a lighter musette sound (slower tremolo beat), and another switch that brings in all three of them for a stronger musette sound (faster tremolo beat). Since I prefer the lighter musette tuning, I would be unlikely to use the third set, so these accordions are not for me. But many people like them, and you may be one. You can evaluate their tuning in the same way you evaluate accordions with just two M sets, except you will make separate evaluations for each switch.

To find the musette accordion that is right for you, you should first listen to lots of accordions, decide which one sounds the best to you, and try to buy one that is tuned very much like it. Learning to recognize and count the tremolo beat, and learning to identify and describe the beat progression will help you describe the tuning you are looking for and will help you recognize it when you hear it.

Drilling down

A complete understanding requires drilling down to see why it takes fewer cents at higher notes to create the desired tremolo beat frequency, so here we go with the explanation.

Any note exactly one octave higher than another note is a tone of exactly twice the frequency of the lower note. Stepping up another octave doubles the frequency again. Consider three A's, each one an octave higher than the previous: A = 220 hertz, A = 440 hertz, and A = 880 hertz. Clearly, there is a difference of 220 hertz between the first pair of A's, while there is a difference of 440 hertz between the second pair. Since there is a greater range of frequencies in the upper octave, yet the same number of notes in each octave, it follows that there must also be a greater frequency difference between any two adjacent notes in the upper octave. That is, the semitone intervals in the higher octave are longer in terms of hertz.

If the semitone intervals at the higher notes contain greater numbers of hertz than at lower notes, then 1/100th of one of those semitone intervals i.e., one cent, must also represent a greater number of hertz. Since each cent represents more hertz at the higher notes and each hertz of difference between the two similar tones generates one bps of tremolo, it follows that each cent also generates more bps of tremolo in the higher notes. If each cent generates more bps of tremolo, then it follows that fewer cents are required at the higher notes to generate any given tremolo beat frequency.

This holds true even when a slower beat is desired at the low end. For example, if we want 1 bps at the low F on our keyboard, we will need to tune the musette reed 1 hertz sharper or flatter than the clarinet reed (I am calling the reed set tuned to concert pitch the clarinet reed set, and I am calling the reed set that is tuned off-pitch to create the tremolo beat the musette reed set). This 1 hertz difference amounts to about 5 cents on an A440 accordion because the frequency of this lowest F in the clarinet set is about 349 hertz, and the frequency of the adjacent F# is about 370 hertz, making the semitone interval about 21 hertz. One cent (1/100th of the semitone interval) is therefore about 0.21 hertz, so 4.76 cents (1 divided by 0.21) is required to achieve a difference of 1 hertz.

If on the same accordion we want a tremolo beat of 6 bps on the highest A in the clarinet set, we will have to tune the corresponding musette reed 6 hertz sharper or flatter than the corresponding clarinet reed. That amounts to about 2.9 cents because at this end of the keyboard the semitone interval is about 209 hertz (A=3520 hertz and A#=3729 hertz, making the difference 209 hertz). One cent (1/100 of 209) is therefore 2.09 hertz, so a 6 hertz difference would equate to 2.87 cents (6 divided by 2.09 is 2.87). Therefore, 2.87 cents of difference will produce exactly the desired tremolo beat of 6 bps.

28.

Proper Care

Now that you have found your accordion, how can you take proper care of it? There are some things you should know.

1. Reed wax melts at 140 degrees Fahrenheit, so if you leave your accordion in your car parked in the hot summer sun with the windows closed, you can expect the wax to melt, allowing some reeds to sag out of place, making the accordion unplayable until costly repairs are made. Don't let your accordion get too hot.

2. Moisture condenses on cold metal parts, so if you move your accordion from a really cold place into a warm room and begin playing it, you can expect moisture to condense on the reeds, causing damage. For instance if you recently chilled the reeds by playing your accordion outdoors on a cold winter day and you subsequently move into a warm room full of moisture-breathing people and start playing it, you will be drawing warm moist air over cold metal reeds. If the temperature of the reeds is below the dew point of the

air, moisture will condense on the cold reeds, causing corrosion that will put the reeds out of tune and perhaps damage them irreparably. If your accordion is really cold, bring it inside and leave it closed tightly in its case (sealed away from moisture) for several hours (as long as it takes for it to warm up nearly to room temperature), before you play it.

3. Salt air is corrosive to reeds and other metal parts, so if you play your accordion at the beach or on your saltwater boat, you can expect the reeds and other metal parts to corrode. Never play your accordion in a salt air environment unless you consider the accordion expendable.

4. Moisture is the enemy of wood and leather, so always keep your accordion in a dry place, and never play it in the rain or fog. Never wash your accordion or keyboard in a manner that might allow any liquid to run or drip into it or under the keys, and never spray any liquid on it. The plastic exterior of your accordion and the buttons and keys can be cleaned with a soft cloth slightly dampened in piano key cleaner. If that does not work, dampen the cloth in rubbing alcohol. <u>Never</u> use acetone, lacquer thinner, or other harsh chemicals, as they will attack and dull the plastic finish.

5. Bass straps are anchored to the accordion with light duty rivets not intended to support the weight of the accordion, so never lift your accordion by the bass strap, or the rivets may fail, causing you

to drop the accordion and damage it. It's okay to lift it by the shoulder straps as long as you are careful not to let a strap get under the edge of a key and bend it up.

6. Your accordion should be kept out of its case in a warm dry room, on a bookshelf or table, and unless it has a tone chamber, it should be resting on its feet (the four feet on the bass plate) with a dust cover over it. In this position all the reed leathers are aligned vertically and are thus less likely to sag away from their reed plates. Nearly as good, from the leathers' point of view, is to keep it in playing position, which at least puts the strong axis of the leathers (the width, rather than the thickness) in opposition to gravity, making them unlikely to sag. The worst position is lying flat with the tops of the keys upward (or downward), because this puts half the leathers in the position where gravity is most likely to cause them to sag away from their reed plates, and they definitely will.

If your accordion has a tone chamber, it is best to store it in playing position, as resting it on its feet would put half the leathers in the tone chamber in the position most likely to cause sagging. This may be why Giulietti used to put a handle on one end of its hard cases in addition to the one between the latches. Standing the case on its end puts the accordion into playing position.

Keeping your accordion out of its case will contribute to its health and longevity if it encourages you to pick it up and play it more often. However, when you transport your accordion, it should be in its case for better protection against bumps and scratches.

7. Accordion case latches are notorious for coming unlatched at inopportune times, so always carry your hard case with the lid toward your leg so if it pops open the lid will hit your leg, rather than your accordion hitting the pavement.

8. When you transport your accordion by car, the best position is with the case handle up, as this has the accordion resting on its feet, well positioned to tolerate any bumps. However, if you think it might tip over going around a curve or during a sudden start or stop, then it is better to place it with the case lid down, so the treble keys and, most importantly, the bass buttons face downward. This is so that if you hit a big bump the bass buttons won't all submerge. If the buttons are facing upward and you hit a big bump, the buttons can submerge into their holes and not come back up, requiring a costly repair.

9. Disuse encourages decay. Storing an accordion for long periods subjects it to possible damage from mildew, moths, and corrosion, and allows leathers to sag and curl back from the reed plates. Accordions should be played regularly. Regularly flushing the inside of the accordion with fresh air by playing it discourages mildew, moths, and corrosion. Playing also flexes the leathers and helps keep them soft and flat against the reed plates.

10. Shoulder strap adjustment is essential to proper playing technique and your health and comfort. The left shoulder strap should

be several inches shorter than the right. Both straps should be adjusted so the accordion sits well to the left of center, putting the black treble keys directly below your chin and the top of the accordion about four inches below your chin. In standing position with your right hand on the keyboard, your right wrist straight, your right elbow slightly raised and straight out to your side, and your right shoulder relaxed (not raised and not pulled to the rear), the finger tips of your right hand should just reach the inboard ends of the black keys. If you find yourself playing with your right shoulder pulled back or raised, or with your right elbow down and/or rearward, or with your right wrist bent, then your accordion is probably too far to the right. If you experience fatigue or pain in your right wrist, elbow, or shoulder, your accordion is probably too far to the right. If you position your accordion properly, you will experience less fatigue and be more likely to play often, which will help keep your accordion in good condition.

11. Not all bellows pins are the same size. They may vary in diameter by 1/1000 inch or more, which can make a difference in how they fit, so when you take them out, keep them in order so they will go back into the same holes. If you inadvertently mix them up, make sure you don't force any of them until you are sure you have the best fit. Forcing the largest pin into the smallest hole may enlarge it, while leaving you with a smaller pin fitting too loosely in the largest hole.

12. Accordions are fragile. If you must ship your accordion, pack it carefully. First immobilize the bass buttons by removing the bass cover and inserting strips of folded cardboard under the bottoms of the pistons to prevent them from moving downward and possibly submerging the buttons. Be sure to advise the recipient on how to remove the cardboard. Wrap the accordion in bubble wrap and put it in its case. Wrap the case in bubble wrap and put it in a tight fitting box. Tape the box well and label it "Fragile - Do not drop." If traveling by airline, never check your accordion as baggage. To protect it from damage, put it in a soft case (or no case so people will see and respect its fragility) and make it your carry-on.

List of Illustrations

Glossary

2/4: An accordion with 2 sets of treble reeds and 4 sets of bass reeds.

3/4: An accordion with 3 sets of treble reeds and 4 sets of bass reeds.

3/5: An accordion with 3 sets of treble reeds and 5 sets of bass reeds.

4/5: An accordion with 4 sets of treble reeds and 5 sets of bass reeds.

5/5: An accordion with 5 sets of reeds on each side.

A440 accordion: An accordion in which the lowest A in the clarinet reed set and the second from lowest A in the bassoon set are tuned to 440 Hz.

A442 accordion: An accordion in which the lowest A in the clarinet reed set and the second from lowest A in the bassoon set are tuned to 442 Hz.

Axle rod: The brass or steel rod on which the treble keys hinge, also commonly called a spindle. The axle rod is as long as the keyboard, and usually about 1.5 mm in diameter. It can usually be accessed from the bottom of the treble keyboard after removing a small metal cover. Full size accordions usually have one axle rod for the black keys and another for the white keys, while many smaller models have all the keys on one axle. Accordions with individually removable keys do not have removable axle rods.

Bass button: One of usually 120 buttons mounted on pistons that activate levers that open valves for each note on the bass side of the accordion.

Bass cabinet: The (usually celluloid covered) wooden case work on the left side of the bellows (from the reference point of the player) to which the bass machine and bass reed blocks are mounted.

Bass cover: A removable wood or metal cover plate over the bass machine.

Bass keyboard: The array of bass buttons on the left side of the accordion that play bass notes and chords.

Bass machine: An assembly of buttons, pistons, levers, bell cranks, cams, and cam followers that act together to open selected bass valves to play the desired individual notes and chords when bass buttons are pushed. Most bass machines must be disassembled piece by piece to gain access to the bass valves, but some accordions have bass machines that can be removed as an assembly, allowing much faster and easier access to the valves.

Bass piston: A metal rod 4 to 6 inches long with a plastic button on top and with 1 to 4 pins protruding from one side which engage levers on bell cranks that open bass note valves when the button is pressed. Note buttons have pistons with just 1 pin for opening just 1 valve, while chord buttons have pistons with 3 or 4 pins to simultaneously open 3 or 4 note valves.

Bass pipes: The bell cranks that open the bass valves. Each pipe is a solid metal rod about 12 inches long which has one cam lever to lift its particular note valve open and several other levers to engage pins on the various bass button pistons that use that note. When such a button is pressed, each of the pins on the piston engages a pipe lever, forcing those pipes to rotate, which in turn causes their cam levers to open their respective valves. In a Stradella bass machine there are two pipes for each bass note on the accordion, one in the chord set and one in the note set, and thus a total of 24 pipes in an accordion which has all the bass notes, i.e., all 12 notes in the chromatic scale.

Bass strap: A 2- to 3-inch wide (usually padded) leather strap on the left side of the accordion used to operate the bellows and to keep the player's arm in position and within easy reach of the bass buttons.

Bass switches: Push-buttons or rockers that operate the bass register slides to control the air flow to each complete set of bass reeds. Bass switches enable the selection of various combinations of bass reed sets.

Bass valve: A wood or metal pallet, usually with felt padding and a leather seal that closes ports for an individual bass note. The bass valve is opened (lifted off its ports) by the action of levers and cams when certain bass buttons are pressed.

Bassoon reeds: The lowest frequency set of treble reeds on the accordion. On a standard accordion this is a set of 41 reeds incorporating all the notes of the chromatic scale from piano F2 to A5.

Bps: Beats per second.

Bellows: A manually operated air pump, constructed mainly of pleated cardboard, which supplies air to the reeds. Pressure on the bellows controls the volume of the sound.

Bellows pin: A short steel nail-like pin that holds the accordion cabinets to the bellows. To inspect the reeds and leathers, the accordion is opened by removing the bellows pins on one side of the bellows and separating the cabinet from the bellows. On each side of the bellows there are usually three pins on the back and three or four in the front, and sometimes one on the top and one on the bottom.

Bellows strap: A leather or metal strap that holds the bellows closed.

Bellows tape: Vinyl faced cloth tape glued over the folds in the bellows to help strengthen the folds, protect them from abrasion, and enhance the appearance.

Castelfidardo: A small city in the Marche region of eastern Italy known for its accordion factories, which produced the vast majority of the accordions found in the United States today. Accordions are still manufactured in Castelfidardo, but on a much smaller scale than fifty years ago.

Clarinet reeds: A set of reeds one octave higher than the bassoon reeds. On a standard accordion this set includes all 41 notes of the chromatic scale from piano F3 to A6.

Choking: Balking. The refusal by a reed to begin vibrating at the sudden onset of air flow, typically caused by inadequate clearance of the reed tongue tip above the plane of the reed plate.

Converter bass: A bass machine that can be switched back and forth between the Stradella and free bass systems.

Dry tuning: No tremolo. All reeds tuned to concert pitch.

Duraluminum: A hard aluminum alloy used in the manufacture of the best reed plates generally used only in handmade reeds.

Foundation plate: The flat wood or metal plate that separates the reed blocks on one side from the valves on the other, and which contains ports under each valve, (and aligned with individual reed chambers in the reed blocks) through which air is allowed to flow when both the register slide and the valve are open. In most accordions the register slides are mounted on the foundation plate under the reed blocks. On the treble foundation plate, one port for each of the treble reed sets is located under each valve. Thus, the number of reed sets can be determined by counting the ports under any treble valve (except in tone chambered accordions, where each key has a second valve in the tone chamber, with one or two of the ports located under that valve).

Free bass: A bass machine in which each bass button operates only one note in only one octave, and in which the buttons are arranged in chromatic scale order through up to five octaves.

Glissando: Sliding a finger up or down the keyboard to sound a series of notes in rapid succession.

Grille: The metal or plastic cover over the treble valves, often incorporating openings for air and sound, which openings are normally covered from the inside by a decorative grille cloth.

Hand fitted reeds: The second highest grade of reeds, with some of the features of handmade reeds, most notably tight clearances between the tongue and the vent.

Handmade reeds: The highest grade of reeds, made from the best materials and incorporating design features that tend to make them more responsive to less bellows pressure, while also remaining more stable frequency-wise under higher bellows pressure. Handmade reeds are the hallmark of the best quality accordions preferred by professional musicians. Fewer than one percent of accordions have handmade reeds.

Hertz: Cycles per second.

Individually removable keys: Treble keys that can be removed without first removing the axle rod. This allows removing any single key without having first to remove all other keys between that key and the end of the axle rod. Many accordions with individually removable keys have a small tool for removing or replacing key springs mounted under the treble grille.

Keyboard: The part of the accordion to which the treble keys are mounted. The term often also includes those keys.

Key rod: The metal extension on the back of each treble key which extends out over the valve ports, and to which the pallet is fixed with either wax, glue, or a plastic sleeve.

LM: An accordion with 1 set of bassoon reeds and 1 set of clarinet reeds.

LMH: An accordion with 1 set of bassoon reeds, 1 set of clarinet reeds, and 1 set of piccolo reeds.

LMM: An accordion with 1 set of bassoon reeds and 2 sets of clarinet reeds.

LMMH: An accordion with 1 set of bassoon reeds, 2 sets of clarinet reeds, and 1 set of piccolo reeds.

LMMM: An accordion with 1 set of bassoon reeds and 3 sets of clarinet reeds.

LMMMH: An accordion with 1 set of bassoon reeds, 3 sets of clarinet reeds, and 1 set of piccolo reeds.

MM: An accordion with 2 sets of clarinet reeds.

MMM: An accordion with 3 sets of clarinet reeds.

Musette reeds: A second and/or third set of clarinet reeds tuned slightly off pitch to create a tremolo effect.

Musette tuning: A tremolo effect achieved by playing two or three reeds for the same note, each of which is tuned to a very slightly different frequency.

Mute: To soften or mellow the sound.

Mute chamber: An enclosure under the treble grille that mutes the sound of the treble reeds. Hinged doors or sliding doors can typically be opened to unmute the reeds.

Pallet: The wood or metal foot on the treble key rod or bass valve which lifts off the ports when a key or button is pressed, allowing air to flow over the reed behind it. The pallet is fitted with a leather seal, often with a felt cushion between the leather valve face and the pallet. The pallet is connected to the key rod or valve lever with reed wax, or sometimes with a plastic sleeve fixed to the pallet which fits snugly over the key rod.

Piccolo reeds: The highest frequency set of reeds available on a standard accordion, one octave higher than the clarinet set, and incorporating all the notes of the chromatic scale from F4 to A7.

Ports: The round or square openings in the foundation plate which allow air flow to be directed over the single reed aligned with each port. A valve opens its ports when the key or button for that particular note is pressed.

Reed: An assembly comprised of 1 reed plate, 2 reed tongues, usually 2 rivets, and usually 2 reed leathers.

Reed blocks: The interior wooden racks that hold the reeds in place over their respective ports and valves. Usually, each full set of treble reeds (41 in most accordions) is split across two reed blocks, one mounted closer to the treble keyboard to house the black key notes in that set, and another mounted farther away to house the white key notes, although space limitations in some designs require two or three of the white key notes to be located in the black key reed block. In some older designs, the register slides are mounted in the reed blocks, while in later designs they are mounted in the foundation plate to which the reed block is mounted. On the bass side, each reed block holds one full set of 12 bass reeds on each side of the block, so each bass reed block can contain up to two complete sets of reeds. Each reed block is divided into small chambers, with one chamber per reed, each chamber being proportional in size to the reed that is mounted to it.

Reed plate: An aluminum (or duraluminum) plate with two long narrow slots in it and with rivet holes for the attachment of two reed tongues, each free to vibrate in one of the slots in response to air flow.

Reed tongue: A spring steel blade riveted to a reed plate. The reed tongue vibrates at a certain frequency when air is forced to flow through the reed.

Reed vent: The slot in the reed plate.

Reed wax: A mixture of mostly beeswax, but also containing some rosin and a bit of linseed oil, which is used to anchor and seal the reed plates to the reed blocks. It is also often used to fasten the pallets to the treble key rods and to the bass valve levers.

Register slides: Thin flat strips of steel or brass approximately 1/2 inch wide x as long as the reed blocks, i.e., 13 to 17 inches long, containing a series of square holes, one hole for each note in the reed block, i.e., one for each valve port. In response to switch movement, the slides slide end-wise to align all the holes with their ports to enable air flow through that set of reeds, or alternatively to close off the ports to disallow air flow through that set of reeds.

Spindle: Treble key axle rod

Stradella bass: The most common type of bass machine, in which the buttons for root notes and their chord families are arranged according to the circle of fifths, and in which each individual note button plays that note in up to five octaves at once, depending on bass switch settings.

Tone chamber: A resonant box of wood or metal to which one or two reed blocks are mounted for the purpose of enhancing the sound emanating from those reeds. On tone chamber accordions, a second set of treble valves operates inside the tone chamber to control those reeds mounted to the chamber. Thus, on tone chamber accordions there are two treble valves attached to each treble key.

Treble cabinet: The (usually celluloid covered) wooden case work on the right hand side of the bellows (from the reference point of the player), to which the treble keyboard, the treble reed blocks, and one side of the bellows are attached.

Treble key: One of usually 41 piano-like keys on the treble side of the accordion.

Treble keyboard: The (usually 41) piano style treble keys and the wooden platform that supports them. The keyboard assembly also includes metal axle rods that run through the keys and the platform, as well as felt cushions under the keys.

Treble switches: Buttons or levers that operate the treble register slides to control the air flow to each complete set of treble reeds. Often, one switch moves two or more register slides simultaneously to enable the selection of various combinations of reed sets.

Treble valve: A wood or metal pallet, usually with felt padding and a leather seal that closes two to four ports for an individual note (the number of ports depends on the number of treble reed sets in the accordion and whether some of those reed sets are mounted to a tone chamber). The pallet and its felt and leather seal are attached to a treble key rod and are lifted off the ports when that treble key is pressed.

Tremolo beat: The slow harmonic frequency generated by two reeds vibrating at nearly the same pitch. The frequency of the tremolo beat is equal to the number of hertz of difference between the two primary frequencies. Thus, if two reeds are tuned n Hertz apart, they will generate a tremolo beat of n beats per second when played together.

Ventilli: Thin flexible plastic reed valves.

Voicing: The adjustment of the clearance of the tip of the reed tongue above the plane of the reed plate to the optimum clearance for rapid response to air flow without choking.

Wet tuning: Musette tuning or tremolo

Accordion Condition Inspection Report   p. 1

Inspection requested by	
Date of inspection	
Accordion description	
Manufacturer/model	
Cabinet Color	
Bellows color	
Size	
Number of treble and bass keys	
Keyboard length	
Reed configuration	
Weight	
Visual inspection - exterior	
General Appearance	
Bellows condition	
Keyboard condition	
Grille condition	
Switches operate properly?	
Shoulder straps condition	
Bass strap condition	
Olfactory inspection	
Odors? Mold, smoke, etc.	
Auditory inspection	
Any silent reeds?	
Any noisey leathers?	
Noisey keyboard?	
Musette Tuning?	
Good reed response?	
General sound quality	
Do microphones work?	

Accordion Condition Inspection Report   p. 2

Tactile inspection

Keyboard length/key spacing	
Keyboard pressure/travel	
Any air leaks?	
Bellows condition	

Visual inspection - under grille

Grille cloth condition	
Treble valve condition	
Key rod condition	
Individually removable keys?	
Switch mechanism condition	
Any microphones?	

Visual inspection - interior

Wax condition	
Leathers condition	
Switches in reed blocks?	
Reed blocks tight and secure?	
Is interior clean?	
Inside of bellows	

Visual inspection - bass machine

button condition	
levers engaged?	
Anything cracked or loose?	
Noisey?	
Bass strap anchor and adj. screw	
Bass grille cloth condition	
Any microphones?	

Case type and condition

Order extra copies of *Piano Accordion Owner's Manual and Buyer's Guide* for your friends.

Your name:	
Street address:	
City:	
State: Zip code:	
Email address: (for communicating re this order. Will not be shared)	

Number of copies:_____ x $25 =

Plus shipping and handling for one copy (U.S. only): $5.00

Plus $.50 S & H for each additional copy

to the same address: $_____

Total enclosed: $

Shipping name and address if different from above:

Mail your order and your check to:

GEORGE BACHICH

ACCORDION REVIVAL

P.O. Box 3238

Napa, CA 94558